SPRINGFIELD CONFIDENTIAL

SPRINGFIELD CONFIDENTIAL

JOKES, SECRETS, AND OUTRIGHT LIES
FROM A LIFETIME WRITING FOR
THE SIMPSONS

MIKE REISS
WITH MATHEW KLICKSTEIN

DEY ST.
An Imprint of WILLIAM MORROW

SPRINGFIELD CONFIDENTIAL. Copyright © 2018 by Reiss Entertainment, Inc. All rights reserved. Printed in the United States of America. No part of this book may be used or reproduced in any manner whatsoever without written permission except in the case of brief quotations embodied in critical articles and reviews. For information, address HarperCollins Publishers, 195 Broadway, New York, NY 10007.

HarperCollins books may be purchased for educational, business, or sales promotional use. For information, please email the Special Markets Department at SPsales@harpercollins.com.

A hardcover edition of this book was published in 2018 by Dey Street, an imprint of William Morrow.

FIRST DEY STREET PAPERBACK EDITION PUBLISHED 2019.

Designed by Michelle Crowe

Library of Congress Cataloging-in-Publication Data has been applied for.

ISBN 978-0-06-274805-8

19 20 21 22 23 LSC   10 9 8 7 6 5 4 3 2 1

To Matt Groening, Jim Brooks, and Al Jean—thanks for the greatest job in the world. Don't fire me.

—Mike Reiss

Welcome to the humiliating world of professional writing.

—Homer Simpson

CONTENTS

ACT THREE

THE TAG

CLOSING CREDITS

FOREWORD

In the early '90s I was a comedian and an aspiring writer. I made my living in three ways: During the day, I worked for Comic Relief, producing benefits for the homeless at comedy clubs, for which I was paid $200 a week. I did stand-up comedy at the Improv and on the road. And I wrote jokes for other comedians, such as Roseanne Barr, Tom Arnold, Jeff Dunham, George Wallace, Taylor Negron, and Garry Shandling.

I was looking for my big break and it was not coming. Some of my friends were able to get jobs as staff writers on the TV show *Roseanne,* but I couldn't seem to make that happen. Some of my other friends, such as David Spade and Rob Schneider, and later Adam Sandler, were hired to be writer/performers on *Saturday Night Live,* but I was never able to get them to hire me. Jim Carrey used to pay me out of his own pocket to write sketches with him for *In Living Color,* but I could never turn that into an official staff job.

I was frustrated and needed to make a move, so I decided to write a spec script, which is basically a sample of writing, in the hopes of getting hired to write for a sitcom. My two favorite television programs at the time were *The Simpsons* and Chris Elliott's *Get a Life.* I sat down over the course of a month or two and wrote one spec episode of each program. At the time, I thought they came out really well, but when I sent them around town, I didn't get hired by any of the shows I applied to and was only able to get one meeting, which was with David Mirkin at *Get a Life*, but I think I only got that meeting because Garry Shandling forced him to meet with me.

The only other feedback I got about my two spec scripts was from Mike Reiss and Al Jean, who were running *The Simpsons*. I was told that they had liked my scripts, but they didn't need any writers at that moment. Even though it was a rejection, it did give me some self-esteem. The writers of my favorite show had said something positive. That wouldn't pay my rent, but it was much better than the reaction I had gotten from every other show on television at the time, which was silence.

Being unable to find a staff job, I started working on a variety of projects, eventually including *The Ben Stiller Show*. After the show was canceled, which was just a few months into our run, I got a call from Mike Reiss who told me that he and Al were creating a new show called *The Critic*, and he wanted to know if I would like to join their staff. I couldn't believe it. He wasn't just being nice when he'd said he liked my *Simpsons* spec. And twenty-two years later, Mike and Al called me and said they wanted to turn that spec into an actual *Simpsons* episode.

I re-read it and it was pretty weak, with a few moments of promise. The fact that Mike could see that promise in me when I was still a kid and that he was excited about it was career-changing for me. I certainly didn't deserve to be in that room. I didn't know anything about writing stories. I hadn't earned my way in. But he saw something in me and was very enthusiastic about my writing and my career. When you're young, you're so thrilled to get a job that you don't think much about what an incredibly giving gesture it is for someone to champion you and open that door for you.

When I was sitting in the writer's room of *The Critic*, I was aware that I was sharing that space with some of the best comedy writers in the world. I was in awe on a daily basis. Most of all, I was in awe of Mike, who was endlessly funny and kind. Always in a great mood, he'd pitch line after line and was so funny that it made me scared to pitch at all, but I forced myself to and got an amazing comedy education from Mike, Al, and James Brooks. I have read and watched everything Mike has created, and he is an inspiration as a brilliant comic mind and as a genuinely fantastic person who has done nothing but make earth a happier place to live. God bless Mike Reiss.

—Judd Apatow

OPENING CREDITS

As good a place as any to start . . .

Since season one, January 1990, each *Simpsons* episode begins with a joke that is missed by tens of millions of fans in hundreds of millions of viewings. When the *Simpsons* title card emerges from the clouds, you see the first half of the family's name, "The Simps," before the rest of the word. *So what?* Well, "Simps," is short for simpletons—stupid people—like the ones you're about to see in the show. If you never caught this, don't feel bad; most of our current staff didn't know it, either.

(Other jokes you may have missed in life: *Toy Story* is a pun on "toy store;" the comedy *Legally Blonde* is a play on that hilarious term "legally blind"; and there's a *31* hidden in the BR logo of Baskin-Robbins, referring to their "31 flavors" slogan. You've already learned four things, and this is just page 1!)

At *The Simpsons,* we put as many jokes in our opening credits as some sitcoms put into an entire episode (or all eight seasons of *Home Improvement).* Our credits always open with a new "chalkboard gag," where Bart writes a phrase repeatedly on the school blackboard, such as "NERVE GAS IS NOT A TOY." And they always close with our "couch gag," where the Simpsons pile onto the sofa and something surprising happens (e.g., the couch eats them).

When the show went to hi-def in 2009, we added more gags: a "fly-by" (some *Simpsons* character zooms past the title in a weird contraption) and a video billboard. Lisa's sax solo in the theme also changes from week to week; lately, it hasn't always been a sax—we've also had her play the harp and theremin.

This whole idea for ever-changing credits came from an unlikely source: the 1950s' *Mickey Mouse Club.* Its opening credits always ended with Donald Duck hitting a gong, and something catastrophic happening: the gong would explode, or Donald would vibrate uncontrollably . . . there were many variations, but they all ended with a duck getting maimed.

Our first chalkboard gag was simple and self-referential: "I WILL NOT WASTE CHALK." Great joke. But it went downhill fast from there: two episodes later the phrase became "I WILL NOT BURP IN CLASS." While there have been plenty of good ones ("BEANS ARE NEITHER FRUIT NOR MUSICAL"), these gags are very hard to write because anything longer than ten words goes by too fast to read. Furthermore, when we drop them from the opening credits, which we do more and more, nobody complains. In fact, sixteen years ago we already had Bart writing on the chalkboard "NOBODY READS THESE ANYMORE."

The couch gags are a lot more fun . . . but a lot more work. We used to repeat every joke once a year, doing eleven couch gags for our twenty-two-episode season. But we quickly learned that if people saw an old couch gag, they thought the whole show was a repeat and tuned out. Now, virtually every episode gets its own couch gag.

Generally, our credit jokes are written at the end of the day. If it looks like work might wrap early, say five thirty P.M., and there's a chance the writers might get home to a hot dinner and nonsleeping children, the boss will tell us to come up with couch gags and chalkboards.

Our couch gags have parodied other shows' opening credits: *The Big Bang Theory*, *Game of Thrones*, and *Breaking Bad*. One time the Simpsons were crushed by the giant foot from the opening credits of *Monty Python's Flying Circus*. Showrunner David Mirkin made sure we used the exact foot Python used: it's from *The Allegory of Venus and Cupid* by Agnolo Bronzino.

A few couch jokes are mini epics. In just seventy seconds, we recapped all of human history, starting with an amoeba that evolves into an ape, then a caveman, then devolves slightly to Homer Simpson. We condensed the *Lord of the Rings* trilogy to a minute thirty-nine.

Sometimes we don't even have to do the work, because guest artists do it for us! This has given us a chance to work with animators we admire, like Bill Plympton, Don Hertzfeldt, and the teams from *Robot Chicken* and *Rick and Morty*. Guillermo del Toro did a three-minute spectacular that referenced every horror movie ever made, and it's simply amazing.

And then there was notoriously reclusive artist Banksy. Al Jean approached him (her? it? them?) through the producer of the Banksy documentary *Exit Through the Gift Shop*. Banksy did a hilariously Orwellian depiction of the Korean animation house where our show is made: in the sequence, *Simpsons* DVDs are pierced on the horn of a starving unicorn to make the center hole, then packed in boxes sealed with a dead dolphin's tongue; live white squirrels are fed into a shredder to make stuffing for Bart dolls, then loaded into a cart pulled by a sickly panda. We loved it; our Korean animators did not. (I was the first *Simpsons* writer to visit our animation house in Seoul; the workers, mostly women, have nicer, sunnier offices than our writers do; and most of them were watching Korean soap operas on their cell phones as they did their jobs.)

My all-time favorite couch gag was the one that aired the night our show beat *The Flintstones* as the longest-running prime-time animated show in history. The Simpsons run into the living room, where they find the Flintstones already sitting on the couch. That show's producers, Hanna-Barbera, asked that the Flintstones be paid as guest cast—and they were! Fred, Wilma, and Pebbles split four hundred bucks.

BURNING QUESTION

Throughout the book, I'll be answering the questions most often asked by *Simpsons* fans.

Let's start with the big one:

Where is Springfield?

The name Springfield was chosen by creator Matt Groening for its generic blandness. It was the name of the hometown in the generically bland 1950s sitcom *Father Knows Best* and is one of the most common place names in America—only Riverside and Five Points beat it. There are forty-eight Springfields in forty-three U.S. states, which means there are five states that have two Springfields. Great imagination, folks.

But Matt Groening's version of Springfield wasn't intended to be a guessing game; like most things on *The Simpsons*, we didn't plan it. And by this point, we've put in enough clues as to where it might be that it can't possibly be *anywhere*. Let's recap what we know: Springfield has an ocean on its east side and its west side. We once said that East Springfield is three times the size of Texas. And in one episode we see Homer shoveling snow in the morning and lying in a hammock sipping lemonade that afternoon. This raises the question: what planet is Springfield on?

The Emmy-winning episode "Behind the Laughter" ends by calling the Simpsons a family from northern Kentucky. There's your answer. Except that in the closed-captioning, we said they're from Missouri. In the rerun, we changed it to Illinois. And it's referred to as "a small island" on the DVD.

In *The Simpsons Movie*, Ned Flanders says that Springfield's state is bordered by Ohio, Nevada, Maine, and Kentucky. There was even a contest to coincide with the release of the movie that invited different Springfields in the United States to make a video explaining why they're the one the Simpsons live in. Thirteen cities entered, competing for the honor of being America's fattest, dumbest, most polluted town. Springfield, Massachusetts's film featured a guest appearance by Senator Ted Kennedy; he invited his soundalike character Mayor Quimby to come visit. This was a big concession by Kennedy, since I've heard that he hated that character. And yet despite all this effort, Massachusetts lost. The winner was Springfield, Vermont. (Comedian Henriette Mantel is from Springfield, Vermont, and she told me it's nothing like the town on the show.)

I like the answer given by John Swartzwelder, the quirky writer of fifty-nine quirky *Simpsons* episodes; he says, "Springfield is in Hawaii." But a few years ago, Matt Groening said the show is set in a city near where he grew up: Springfield, Oregon. What does he know?

ACT ONE

I hope this book feels like a *Simpsons* episode: fast-paced, full of quick scenes, and stuffed with hundreds of jokes, some of them funny. I've even structured it like a *Simpsons* script, which has four acts: setup, complication, resolution, and coda. Now, Aristotle said all drama has three acts, and classic films usually employ a three-act structure. We have four, which means we're one act better than Aristotle. Also, with four acts, you can sell more commercials.

The Simpsons has a structure like no other show that preceded it. The first act of every episode kicks off with a string of scenes that have nothing to do with the plot of the show: it may be a visit to a water park, a trip to the stamp museum, a visit to an *indoor* water park . . . we're kinda running out of ideas. It isn't till the end of act 1 that the story really presents itself, though it's barely connected to what came before: Homer fights with Marge in a movie theater and winds up managing a country-western singer; making funeral arrangements for Grampa becomes a story about the Simpsons getting a tennis court; Lisa becomes a veterinarian after . . . a visit to a water park.

The first act of this book will be like that: there's a point to it all, but you'll never see it coming.

CHAPTER ONE

IT BEGINS . . .

I got the *Simpsons* job the same way I got a wife: I was not the first choice, but I was available.

I was working at *It's Garry Shandling's Show*, the second-lowest-rated show on TV. (The lowest-rated was *The Tracey Ullman Show*, which featured short cartoons about these ugly little yellow people.) The Shandling show was going on summer break and showrunner Alan Zweibel was launching a new show, *The Boys*, a sitcom set at the Friars Club. Man, I wanted that job, where I would have been writing jokes for Norm Crosby and Norman Fell, two of my favorite Normans!

But Zweibel opted to hire my old friends Max Pross and Tom Gammill, so my writing partner, Al Jean, and I had to settle for the job they turned down: *The Simpsons*.

Nobody wanted to work on *The Simpsons*. There hadn't been a cartoon in prime time since *The Flintstones*, a generation before. Worse yet, the show would be on the Fox network, a new enterprise that no one was even sure would last.

I took the job . . . but didn't tell anyone what I was doing. After eight years writing for films, sitcoms, and even Johnny Carson, I was now working on a cartoon. I was twenty-eight years old and I thought I'd hit rock bottom.

Still, I'd been a fan of Matt Groening and executive producer Sam Simon for years. They were having fun creating the show, and it was infectious. It was a summer job and it felt like the summer jobs I'd had in the past (selling housewares, filing death certificates): we knew we wouldn't be doing this forever, so no one took it too seriously. We didn't even have a real office at the time. The studio had so little faith in us, they housed us in a trailer. I assumed that if the show failed, they'd slowly back the trailer up to the Pacific and drown the writers like rats.

Al Jean and I quickly churned out three of the first eight episodes of the show: "There's No Disgrace Like Home," which ends with the Simpsons electrocuting each other during family therapy; "Moaning Lisa," in which a depressed Lisa meets jazz great Bleeding Gums Murphy; and "The Telltale Head," where Bart saws the head off the Jebediah Springfield statue. This is also the episode in which Sideshow Bob, Reverend Lovejoy, Krusty the Clown, and bullies Jimbo, Dolph, and Kearney first appear.

But the whole time I was writing, I groused, "I'd rather be doing jokes for Norman Fell." Since so few writers wanted to work on the series, we wound up with a very eclectic writing staff: except for Al and me, none of them had ever written a sitcom script before. They'd come from the world of sketches, late-night TV, even advertising. One day before the series premiered, I was sitting in the trailer with the other writers. After Matt Groening left the room, I asked the question that was on all our minds: "How long do you actually think this show will last?"

Every writer had the same answer. Six weeks. Six weeks, six weeks, six weeks. Only Sam Simon was optimistic. "I think it will last thirteen weeks," he said. "But don't worry. No one will ever see it. It won't hurt your career."

Maybe that's the secret of the show's success: since we thought no one would be watching, we didn't make the kind of show we saw on TV; we made the kind of show we wanted to see on TV. It was unpredictable; one week we wrote a whodunit, and in another we parodied the French film *Manon of the Spring*. The only rule was one we made for ourselves—don't be boring. The scenes were snappy and packed with jokes, in the dialogue, in the foreground, and in the background. When Homer went to a video arcade in episode 6, Al and I filled the place with funny games like *Pac-Rat*, *Escape from Grandma's House*, and *Robert Goulet Destroyer*. And if you missed a joke the first time, no problem; everyone in America was starting to get VCRs, so they could tape the show and watch it again.

Remember, this was 1988, and the number one TV series was *The Cosby Show*. It was a great show . . . but it was slooooow. Nothing ever happened on *The Cosby Show*. (A lot happened after *The Cosby Show* . . .)

It's no joke to say that the fastest-paced, most irreverent comedy on TV around this time was *The Golden Girls*, a show about three corpses and a mummy. (I broke into sitcoms writing a script for *The Golden Girls*. Now I *am* one.)

DAN CASTELLANETA ON *THE SIMPSONS'* PROSPECTS

"When I read the first script, I was blown away. I really thought it was well written. I didn't know whether or not the show would be successful, but if we only had thirteen episodes, we would at least have a cult following. The scripts were that good."

Sam Simon taught me everything I know. About boxing.

The Simpsons Speak

After a year spent preparing thirteen scripts, it was time for a table read. This is when the writers and producers get together in a conference room to hear the actors perform the script for the first time. It's probably the most important part of the process. How do the characters sound and interact? Does the story flow? Do the jokes get laughs from the fifty or sixty people in the room?

Our first table read was in early 1989—it was the first time the *Simpsons* cast was gathered in one place, the first time they acted out a full episode of the show. I recognized Dan Castellaneta (Homer) from *The Tracey Ullman Show*; as for Julie Kavner (Marge), I'd had a crush on her since she played Brenda Morgenstern on *Rhoda*. Still do. Even though I'd cowritten three episodes by this point, I had no idea the children's voices were done by adult women. I'd assumed Bart was played by a young boy, not thirty-two-year-old Nancy Cartwright; it was even weirder that Yeardley Smith, a grown woman, barely changed her voice to play Lisa Simpson.

Oh, that poor girl, going through life stuck with that voice, I thought. That "poor girl" has since earned an Emmy and $65 million with that voice.

Hank Azaria hadn't been cast yet; at that time, his character Moe was played by comedian Christopher Collins. (When Hank was later hired, he went back and re-recorded all of Moe's lines). Cartoon legend June Foray (Rocky the Flying Squirrel!) also did a few parts at that first reading, but she sounded too cartoony for our show. A local radio personality played psychiatrist Dr. Marvin Monroe, but he was fired at the end of the reading. (We later killed off the character of Marvin Monroe. And the real radio shrink we based him on committed suicide. All in all, kind of a cursed character.)

Comedy writer Jerry Belson, considered one of the funniest men in the world, was brought in to punch up the script with new jokes. He offered only one: a psychiatric patient we described as "Nail-biter (not his own)" was changed by Jerry to "Bedwetter (not his own)."

I didn't realize what a momentous occasion this table read was because, frankly, it wasn't. The whole thing played a little flat. Kind of slow. A few laughs. No one would ever have guessed from that first table read that we'd be doing six hundred more of them. The prospects for *The Simpsons* weren't great, and they were about to get even bleaker . . .

We Almost Get Canceled . . . Before We Come On

Fox had to take a giant leap of faith when the network picked up *The Simpsons* for the first season. With an animated show, a studio can't just do a pilot and then decide later to pick up the rest of the series. It's prohibitively expensive to make only one episode of a cartoon. Animation is also a slow process: there would be a one-year gap between the pilot and the first episode. By that time, half the network executives who'd bought the show would have been fired, forced out of the business, and possibly become fugitives from justice.

So Fox had to pick up a whole season of *The Simpsons* and paid something like $13 million for thirteen episodes without seeing one frame of animation.

Our first finished, full-color episode, the pilot, "Some Enchanted Evening," had just come in from overseas. While our basic creative animation is done in Hollywood, the actual drawing and hand-painting of over twenty-four thousand cels in each episode is done in Korea. South Korea. The nice Korea. The plot of the pilot has the notorious Babysitter Bandit trying to rob the Simpsons' house while Homer and Marge are having a romantic night away from the kids.

When the writers and Fox executives got together and watched it, they thought it was *terrible*. A total disaster. The script was clumsy—pilots often are—but it was the animation that felt completely wrong: the Simpson house was bendy, Homer was wiggly, all of Springfield seemed to be made of rubber.

When the screening ended there was dead silence. The small audience in attendance gaped at the screen like it was the first act of *Springtime for Hitler*. Someone had to break the silence. Finally, writer Wally Wolodarsky shouted with ironic glee, "Show it again!"

Fox was up in arms. It's possible this would have been the end of *The Simpsons*. But the next week, a second episode, "Bart the Genius," came in, where Bart cheats on an IQ test and ends up getting sent to a school for gifted children—and *that* episode, thankfully, was just great. It was directed with a sure hand by David Silverman, and the script was by one of our best writers, Jon Vitti. It reaffirmed everybody's faith in the series.

This forced us into switching around the original order of how the episodes were to be aired. And so *The Simpsons* premiered, three months late, with episode 9, "Simpsons Roasting on an Open Fire," as a Christmas special. "Bart the Genius" would be the first regular episode; and the original pilot became our season finale, giving us time to fix the animation.

In December 1989, we had a premiere party for the Christmas show in a bowling alley. It was pretty low-rent as premiere parties go, but then Fox wasn't eager to throw more money at our expensive little series.

And then, at eight P.M., the show aired. We all stopped bowling to watch it on overhead monitors. And . . . it was funny, touching, smart, and sweet; none of us saw it coming.

Soon after, someone from Fox's publicity team came in with a packet of reviews from newspapers across the country: the critics not only loved the show, they recognized it as "ground-breaking," and a "game-changer." The next morning, we learned that *The Simpsons* had debuted to the highest rating in the history of the Fox network. We were a success right out of the gate, and we were all over the moon. Except for one man.

Sam Simon stood at the back of the bowling alley, flipping through the packet of reviews with a wry smile on his face. At last, he said with a rueful laugh, "They don't mention me once."

It's not as petty as it may sound. *The Simpsons* was the greatest thing Sam had done in an already great career that included *Taxi* and *Cheers*. Sam had hired all the *Simpsons* writers, set the tone of the show, worked out all the stories, and supervised every script . . . and, to his surprise, Matt Groening got all the acclaim.

Matt never hogged the credit. Whenever he did an interview, he would mention all of us by name. When he went on *The Tonight Show*, I remember, he kept bringing up the other writers . . . but Jay Leno cut him off.

Why?

The Simpsons' premiere party, at a bowling alley, in 1989. Me; my wife, Denise; and Sam Simon's first wife, actress Jennifer Tilly. This was the night everything fell apart.

It made for a great story: "TV is being changed by this *underground cartoonist* who's breaking all the rules. . ." instead of "TV's been changed by an underground cartoonist . . . *and* a veteran TV producer (Sam Simon)."

And so *The Simpsons* was launched. The public loved us. The critics loved us. And the creators were beginning to hate each other.

Simpsonsmania!

Months after our premiere, *The Simpsons* was not just in the papers every day; it was in every section of the newspaper! News, Entertainment, Sports, Business: editors realized a cartoon of Bart was more eye-catching than, say, a photo of Secretary of State Lawrence Eagleburger. And 90 percent of what I read about *The*

Simpsons was wrong, which made me realize 90 percent of everything I read in the paper was probably wrong.

Example: When blues guitarist Stevie Ray Vaughan died in a helicopter crash, one newspaper reported that his last act had been to record a song for the upcoming *The Simpsons Sing the Blues* album. In truth, Mr. Vaughn's last act was to say something like "Fuck *The Simpsons*! I'm not recording a song for their stupid album."

In 1990, Matt Groening wound up on a list as one of the ten most admired men in America, while Sam Simon was the answer to a trivia question on a *Simpsons* bubble gum card. The world kept forcing all the credit on Matt, and it made Sam miserable. He could be a wraith in the office, stomping around like Salieri in *Amadeus*.

Sam was still running the show and turning out classic scripts; he could be great fun to be around. But when Matt came into the room Sam would glower at him and make nasty asides till Matt walked out.

I sympathized with Sam, but I felt bad for Matt, too. Here was the crowning achievement of his life . . . and he was unwelcome in his own office. One day, I went to Matt privately and told him, "Not everybody hates you."

When Matt told Sam a writer had said that, Sam got furious: *You're lying! Who was it?* I never fessed up and I never will.

Oh crap! I just did.

Amazingly, Sam turned his bitterness into a great episode. He pitched a story where Homer, like Sam, creates something truly extraordinary . . . and Moe gets all the credit for it. Homer becomes twisted with rage and destroys them both. The show is called "Flaming Moe's" and is considered one of the best *Simpsons* episodes ever.

This cold war went all the way through the first two seasons. By the end, Sam and Matt were not talking, casting a pall over what should have been happy, glorious years. So how was it resolved? They told Sam to stop running the show, and put two saps in charge: me and Al Jean. Up until that point, the biggest thing I'd ever run was a dishwasher.

AL JEAN ON TAKING OVER
THE SIMPSONS

"Mike and I were so intimidated because we knew this was a great show, a classic. We had left *ALF* after season 2, and by season 4 it was already off the air. So I was really scared that if *The Simpsons* was canceled while we were running it, we'd be blamed for ruining this incredible thing. And there was a history of shows that appeal mostly to kid audiences, like *Mork & Mindy* or *ALF,* that shoot up and then shoot back down very quickly. They become evanescent. So Mike and I worked on *The Simpsons* nonstop to make sure that didn't happen to us."

Who's the Genius?

Decades after the Matt and Sam conflicts, fans still ask: who's the one genius responsible for *The Simpsons*? It's a show with twenty writers, dozens of animators, forty-seven producers, and ten regular or semiregular voice actors, but everyone wants to find the *one guy* responsible. It's understandable—everyone loves a hero story.

For years, the title went to Matt Groening. He did, after all, create the little buggers. Then the honor shifted to Sam Simon, and then to writer George Meyer, after he was written up in *The New Yorker,* that gut-bustingly funny magazine. Strangely, no one has ever given the credit to me . . . including me.

Who's the genius? My answer to the question narrows it down to three people. Actually four. No, five. Make that thirteen.

Matt Groening definitely created the Simpsons, and the story of how he did it is truly unbelievable. Matt was a Los Angeles underground cartoonist when he was called in for a meeting at *The Tracey Ullman Show*. The series had one-minute animated bumpers (as well as live novelty acts), but no one was particularly enamored with them. Matt was told this was a "get-acquainted meeting"—he wasn't expected to pitch anything. But shortly before the meeting, someone said to him, "We're very excited to hear about your new project!" Matt didn't have one. And so, five minutes before the meeting, he sketched out the Simpson family.

It took him five minutes to create one of the most-honored shows in TV history. Just imagine if he'd spent half an hour.

How did he come up with it so fast? For starters, he named the characters after his family: his parents, Homer and Marge; his sisters Lisa and Maggie. He claims Bart is just an anagram of *brat,* but I think the name may have been inspired by his brother, Mark.

The Simpsons shorts are crudely made—so crude, in fact, that they've never been released on DVD; so crude that even Fox has never tried to make a buck on them. But they quickly evolved, thanks to Matt's graphic genius. He once told me, "The key to the Simpsons is that each character is recognizable in silhouette." It's an amazing insight, one I never heard from any other cartoonist. In the earliest days of the show, when we'd be screening rough animation, he'd stop tape every few seconds: "I hate those lines around Bart's eyes! That napkin holder is too small!" I thought he was nuts, but watching those old shows now, I see that he was creating the precise look of the show as he went along. Also, the napkin holder *was* too small.

When the call came to turn the shorts into a half-hour series, Matt was paired with Sam Simon. Sam was a TV prodigy, having run the show *Taxi* at age twenty-three, before moving on to

Cheers and *It's Garry Shandling's Show*. Sam supervised the writing of *The Simpsons*' first two seasons and developed the show's signature mix of highbrow and low, all moving at warp speed.

So if Matt is Thomas Edison inventing the lightbulb, Sam is George Westinghouse, building the factory to crank the bulbs out.

Then there's James L. Brooks. (I call him Jim—you don't get to.) Jim gave the characters soul and pitched the long, heartfelt monologues that gave the Simpsons unexpected depth. To continue the metaphor, Jim Brooks gave the lightbulb heart. Okay, let's drop the metaphor.

There's a simple mnemonic to remember it all: Matt did the art; Sam made it smart; Jim gave it heart. Easy, but wrong, because Matt and Jim also pitch great jokes, and Sam was no slouch at art. He was a college cartoonist who went on to design Mr. Burns and Bleeding Gums Murphy.

Speaking of art, let's not forget David Silverman, the animation supervisor of the show for decades. He first pitched the idea to Jim of turning the one-minute Simpsons shorts into a half-hour show. David had to reinvent how to produce a weekly animated series—it had been twenty years since *The Flintstones* was in prime time, and no one remembered how it was done. Silverman refined the style of the show and set a high standard for the animation. (Even as a kid watching *The Flintstones* I thought, "They keep running past the same goddamn palm tree!") David had brilliant animators working under him, including future Oscar winners Brad Bird (*Ratatouille, The Incredibles*) and Rich Moore (*Zootopia*).

And we can't ignore Al Jean, who has had the soul-crushing job of showrunner on *The Simpsons* for twenty of its thirty seasons. Nor can you forget our six main cast members—Dan Castellaneta, Julie Kavner, Nancy Cartwright, Yeardley Smith, Hank Azaria, and Harry Shearer—who created the voices of not only the Simpson family but the other two hundred residents of Springfield as well.

That's the answer—those thirteen men and women are the one guy who is most responsible for *The Simpsons*.

That's All, Folks!

In 1993, midway through season 4, Sam Simon was asked to leave the show he helped create; in 2015, he passed away at the young age of fifty-nine. He retained his executive producer credit (and salary) on *The Simpsons* through the end of his life, although he hadn't worked on the show, or even set foot in the office, for more than two decades. As for Matt, *Futurama* later proved that even without Sam's help he could create a smart, visionary show.

In the end, Sam got over his anger, saying, "I've gone from getting too little credit for *The Simpsons* to too much." Matt said something similar to *LA Weekly* in 2007: "I'm one of those people who gets more credit than I deserve."

There you have it: the one dark secret of our show, the lone bruise on the *Simpsons* banana. That's all the gossip I've got. (Okay, there's a little bit more ugliness in chapter 12, during the *Simpsons/Critic* crossover.)

Maybe that's the key to the show's longevity—there's no drama at our comedy show. *The Simpsons* keeps rolling along because everyone gets along: the cast, the animators, and the writers all respect each other. There are still plenty of stories and secrets to tell about the show, but if you want dirt, dig a hole.

Now, let's step back a little to how I got here . . .

CHAPTER TWO

A BRIEF HISTORY OF ME

I was recently reading about myself on IMDb, because, well, who else would? In a discussion thread titled "Mike Reiss Simpsons DVD Commentaries," someone posted, "This guy sounds like he's smiling all the time."

That made me smile.

The next post read, "Yeah. It really gets on my nerves."

I stopped smiling. But screw that guy. If I do smile a lot, it's because I have the funnest job in the world. And because I have a beautiful wife who laughs at all my jokes. And because I think *funnest* is a word.

As a child I spent my first three years sitting in my playpen, never saying a word, just grinning like an idiot. My mother finally took me to a doctor, who told her, "The boy's not brain-damaged. He's just a little slow."

Let's chalk it up to the fact that I found life amusing, even at that age. I believe I was making up jokes for other babies, like "My daddy breastfeeded me." (Hey, that's not bad!) But to best understand my upbringing, you have to start with a joke. A joke about jokes:

A convict stands up in the prison mess hall and yells, "Seventy-three!" All the other inmates laugh. A new prisoner asks a guard what's going on. The guard explains that the prison has one joke book and all the prisoners have memorized it. So instead of telling the joke, they just say the number of it. So the new prisoner stands up and yells, "Forty-eight!"

He gets no response and asks the guard why. The guard says to him, "Some guys know how to tell 'em, some guys don't."

My childhood was like this prison. I grew up in a house full of funny people who all loved jokes. We studied the four-hundred-page *Joey Adams Joke Dictionary* the way Quaker families study the Bible. In fact, none of us had to tell a whole joke. We'd just mention a joke fragment, like "elephant-ear sandwich," and everyone would laugh.[*]

I grew up in suburban Connecticut, the middle child of five kids. I have a brother who dabbled in stand-up comedy and a sister who wrote a joke book for speech therapists entitled *How many speech-language pathologists does it take to change an audiologist?* (It's got five stars on Amazon.)

I was a pretty funny kid, too. One day, my mother heard that our handsome cousin was marrying a hunchback. She asked, "Why would he do that?"

I said, "For good luck!" My father, normally a gentle man, smacked me in the head.

When I turned ten, I offered my Hungarian grandmother a

---

[*] A deli has a sign that reads WE MAKE ANY KIND OF SANDWICH. So a wise guy says, "Okay, I'd like an elephant-ear sandwich." The waiter goes into the kitchen and returns a moment later. "We can't do it," he says. "The boss won't kill a whole elephant for just one sandwich."

slice of my birthday cake. She said, in her Yoda-like old-Jewish-lady syntax, "I only want next year you should give me a piece."

I replied, "It'll be stale by then."

My father smacked me again. I began to think a joke was not truly good unless someone got hit for telling it.

My dad—a physician, a historian, a Phi Beta Kappa scholar—had a little bit of Homer Simpson in him. All dads do. You know, that mixture of anger, love, frustration, and more anger. Matt somehow found the character in his own father, Homer Groening, a documentary filmmaker who surfed and, ironically, had a full head of hair. (Sam Simon developed the character by drawing on *his* father, a man who seems to have little in common with Homer: he was a one-legged Jewish millionaire from Beverly Hills.)

My father's mother may have been the funniest one in the family. I once asked her, after reading a Dixie cup riddle, "What's worse than finding a worm in an apple?"

The cup's answer was "Finding half a worm in an apple."

My grandma Rosie's answer? "Having someone shove an umbrella up your tuchis . . . and then open it."

That was a better answer. And she came up with it so fast I thought it must have happened to her. Maybe it was the Cossacks. Maybe it was Grampa.

My other grandmother summed up our family best. Grandma Mickey was a South Carolina Jew (which is sort of like being a Baptist). After a family dinner one night she said, "Y'all make so many jokes!" Then, after a beat, she added: "Of course, none of them are worth a damn."

Bristol, Connecticut, was a factory town that didn't make things—we made the things that went into other things: brass, springs, and ball bearings. Ask anyone from Bristol what it's like and they'll say, "It's like the town from *The Deer Hunter*." I was never sure whether they meant Bethlehem, Pennsylvania, or Saigon.

But to me, Bristol represented Springfield. I've used so much of what I saw growing up as inspiration for *The Simpsons*. One of the very first scenes in the first episode of the show has Homer losing a game of Scrabble to his son and then throwing the whole game into the fireplace. My friend's father did that. His name was Mr. Burns, by the way: Larry Burns. Years later, we did an episode where Monty Burns's illegitimate son shows up (gloriously voiced by Rodney Dangerfield). By coincidence, the episode writer Ian Maxtone-Graham named the character Larry Burns. By an even greater coincidence, the artists designed a character that looked exactly like my friend's father.

I told the real Larry Burns that we had named and designed the character just like him. He seemed totally unimpressed; nobody cared about show biz in Bristol. But after he died, I found out that my Larry Burns had bought up every Larry Burns *Simpsons* collectible figure in America. Perhaps he was building a clone army.

Like many comedy writers, I was inspired at a young age by *The Dick Van Dyke Show*. But I didn't want to be Dick, handsome TV head writer, married to perky Mary Tyler Moore. I wanted to be Morey Amsterdam, the funny little guy on the show with the big blond wife, who cracked a lot of jokes at the office but didn't do much work.

I have achieved all my childhood goals.

I loved movies, too, and was obsessed with the Marx Brothers. Nothing unique there. I was also fascinated by one of their writers, Al Boasberg, the great "script doctor." It was said that Boasberg couldn't write a great screenplay, but he was a genius at punching up other people's work. Somehow I knew that's what I was destined to do: not to be a writer but to be a rewriter. And when my parents' friends asked me what I wanted to be when I grew up, I'd tell them script doctor.

"Oh, isn't that cute," they'd say. "He wants to be a doctor like his daddy."

"Not a doctor, you country-fried idiots. A script doctor!" I'd mutter.

My writing career began in third grade. My teacher, Miss Borwerk, inspired the first poem I ever wrote:

I have a teacher named Miss Borwerk
Every day she gives me more work

All right, it's not Emily Dickinson, but I was eight, for chrissake.

Whenever I came home from school, my mother would ask me what had happened in class that day. I'd say, "Nothin'." And my mom said, "'Nothing' didn't happen in school today! Tomorrow, when you come home, you better have something to tell me."

Well, the next day nothing happened in school. When my mom asked me about my day, I panicked. In desperation I said, "Today a dog walked into class and Miss Borwerk threw it out the window."

This seemed to satisfy her. So the next day, when nothing happened in school, I told her, "Today Miss Borwerk shot at the kids with paintballs."

And the next day: "Miss Borwerk took off her underwear in front of the class."

What I didn't realize was that my mother believed these stories! She called the principal and said, "You have a teacher there named Miss Borwerk who's a lunatic."

When the principal reprimanded Miss Borwerk for taking off her underwear in class, Miss Borwerk protested, "I don't wear underwear." In turn, Miss Borwerk yelled at the principal, the principal yelled at my mother, and my mother should have yelled at me. Instead, she bought me a pencil box and a pad of paper, and said, "From now on, if you're going to make up stories, write them down."

I've been making up stories ever since . . .

Including that whole thing about Miss Borwerk. Never happened.

Psych!

The next three teacher stories are absolutely true, but, God, I wish they weren't:

I had a teacher who liked my writing and told me to "follow my dreams." A year later he was busted by the vice squad for following *his* dreams.

Another teacher told me, "Be what you always wanted to be." I ran into him six years later in a Boston salad bar. He was my busboy. Maybe that was what he "always wanted to be." But it raised an interesting philosophical question: how much do you tip the man who changed your life?

Answer: 17 percent.

Finally, there was Mrs. Defeo, my faculty adviser, who would hack my high school newspaper articles to pieces and change all my punchlines. This was excellent training for a career in television.

I once wrote a parody of our Student of the Month column. That month's winner was a clearly psychotic kid who suggested we change the school colors to "black and darker black."

Mrs. Defeo changed it to "black and blue." "I can't believe you missed the obvious joke!" she said.

"That's why I didn't do it!" I cried. "It's the obvious joke!"

"You'll never get a job writing for *Cracked* magazine with that attitude."

Every night I'd pray to God that he'd punish Mrs. Defeo for her crimes against comedy.

A year later, she won a million dollars in the Connecticut lottery.

God always listens to my prayers, then does the exact opposite.

This was a rough-and-tumble public high school, and I was the only Jewish kid out of sixteen hundred students. And yet still, my mother said, "I only want you to date Jewish girls."

I said, "Well, Mom, it looks like it's going to have to be you."

So I dated my mom for a few months. We got along fine, but her kids hated me.

In 1990, when I won my first Emmy for *The Simpsons,* I had my wife take a picture, which I sent to my hometown newspaper. Three days later, that photo of me in a tuxedo clutching an Emmy appeared on the front page of the local paper. The caption read LOCAL MAN CLAIMS TO WIN AWARD.

On to Harvard

If a giant sinkhole opened up and swallowed Harvard University, I'd think, *Poor sinkhole.* I spent four years at Harvard and I hated the place. I'm not alone: In a 2006 poll, the *Boston Globe* ranked schools in terms of fun and social life. Harvard came in fifth . . . from the bottom. Amazing. I couldn't imagine four schools *less fun* than Harvard. But then I saw the list. The four schools ranked below us were:

- 🍺 Guantanamo Tech
- 🍺 Chernobyl Community College
- 🍺 The University of California at Aleppo, and
- 🍺 Cornell

At Harvard, the professors were dispassionate and their classes esoteric (though they did teach me the words "dispassionate" and "esoteric"). In four years there, I learned three things:

1. How to open a champagne bottle

2. How to make a bong out of an apple

3. That mayonnaise is delicious (we didn't have it in my house growing up)

I went into college knowing Latin and calculus. After four years, I'd forgotten them both. Blame the apple bong for that.

I tried to have fun at Harvard. In my freshman year, I did stand-up in the school talent show. After the performance, the judge told me, "You're pretty funny." So I married her. That's the last time I ever did stand-up.

There was only one other comedian in the talent show, a guy named Paul, who bombed terribly:

PAUL: Coming up next, survivors of *The Texas Chain Saw Massacre* will form a human pyramid.

AUDIENCE: Booo!

After the show, I told him, "Paul, maybe comedy's not your thing." He took my advice, went into drama, and created the hit medical show *House*. Paul is now worth a zillion dollars; me, I still steal Splendas from KFC.

In short, there are just two things I took from Harvard that I treasure to this day: my beautiful wife, Denise, and a large pile of library books. They're both stacked in the bedroom.

AUDIENCE: Booo!

My wife and I visit the Harvard Lampoon Building. The building was designed by *Lampoon* founder Edmund March Wheelwright; it's said he built it either just before or right after he went mad. Funds for the project came from *Lampoon* alum William Randolph Hearst.

The *Harvard Lampoon*

Why did I even go to Harvard? I only knew two facts about the place before enrolling:

1. Thurston Howell III, the clueless millionaire from *Gilligan's Island,* went there. (My freshman roommate was Thurston Howell IV.)

2. It had a humor magazine, the *Harvard Lampoon.* I wanted to be part of it.

Back in the 1970s the *Lampoon* was not known as an incubator for comedy writers. In fact, for its first century of existence, it produced only four famous graduates: Robert Benchley, George Plimpton, John Updike, and Fred Gwynne, the guy who played Herman Munster (really!). In comedy terms, that list of famous alumni consists of a funny guy, a wry guy, a serious guy, and Frankenstein.

The legacy of the *Lampoon* changed when a member named Jim Downey got hired on the first season of *Saturday Night Live* (and stayed there for four decades). Jim opened the door to two more *Lampoon* friends, who let in some more friends, and by the end of the millennium, there were dozens of Lampooners in movie and TV comedy. Jim Downey was like a funny Patient Zero. There are so many of us working in Hollywood that we're called the *Lampoon* Mafia, which is kind of an insult . . . to the Mafia. At least they have a code of honor.

At the 2016 Emmys, four of the six nominated comedy series were run by *Lampoon* alums (*Veep, Silicon Valley, Master of None, Unbreakable Kimmy Schmidt),* and the last two series were created by Lampooners as well. In the best comedy script category, four of the five nominees, including the winner, were written by our graduates.

Lampoon people are everywhere, working on, sometimes running, every late-night show (*Fallon, Kimmel, Corden, Colbert, The Daily Show,* and, obviously, *Conan*). They've made up 30 percent or more of the writers of the seminal comedies of the recent past: *Seinfeld, SNL, Letterman,* and *The Office.* And, in animation, you'll find them working for *Bob's Burgers, Futurama, Family Guy,* and, of course, *The Simpsons.* Our original writing staff, hired by Stanford grad Sam Simon, was half Lampooners. Since then, about forty more Harvard grads have worked on the show, including eleven *Lampoon* presidents.

But how does a magazine founded in the nineteenth century prepare writers for a career in TV? Because, by a pure accident of history, the competition to get on the *Lampoon* operates exactly like the TV business. Students competing (called "compers") are expected to turn in six humorous articles in eight weeks, which teaches you to hit deadlines and to be prolific, two fundamental skills in television. Like in TV, the competition is brutal—every year, about a hundred writers try out, and only seven get chosen. And finally, just like in TV, the process is completely unfair—very few compers get elected their first time. I had to go through the process twice; Dave Mandel, the brilliant showrunner who year after year takes *Veep* to an Outstanding Comedy Series Emmy, went through it five times. Comedy legend Al Franken was turned down by the magazine, which shows it's easier to get elected to (and subsequently booted out of) the U.S. Senate than to get on the *Harvard Lampoon.* To join the magazine, you need to be self-confident, dedicated, and a little bit delusional. Just like a TV writer.

Once you get on a staff, whether it's the *Lampoon* or a sitcom, you're doing the same thing: sitting on your ass in a room full of funny people, eating crap food. In both cases, you shoot the breeze all day (and long into the night), making jokes and mastering the skill of fast, funny banter.

The one paradox is that while Lampooners write great TV, their magazine sucks. I've never understood why, but the *Harvard Lampoon* is bad today, it was bad when I was president, and it was bad when Robert Benchley ran it. For the half century before him, it was bad *and* racist. You can read all about it in my next book, *Fifty Years of Laughter: A Hundred and Forty Years of the* Harvard Lampoon.

CONAN O'BRIEN'S *HARVARD LAMPOON* DINNER

"Mike and Al showed up at the *Lampoon* and we had a big dinner for them. It was not even my idea, but I think the chef thought it would be really funny that since I was the president of the *Lampoon,* they would just serve potatoes for dinner. That's all there was: potatoes. And I remember Al Jean and Mike Reiss being really pissed because they had legitimately come here for a meal. We treated the meal as a funny conceptual thing, and they were like, 'Where's my fucking lobster?' We were like, 'Well, no, this is the comedy, you see?' And they were like, 'No, we're adults and this is supposed to be a meal, and we're hungry.' So they didn't forgive me for that for a while. For *years* afterward, Mike Reiss was mad about that potato dinner. I think he got back at me, though, because I went to his apartment in New York a few years ago, and he served me some Manischewitz out of a box that I think had been sitting in the sun since the Ford administration. So, he got me back."

(AUTHOR'S NOTE: I thought that was good wine.)

Harvard Lampoon, 1981. (Left to right:) That's me and Al Jean in the front. Behind us, future attorney Ted Phillips and future Futurama writer Pat Verrone.

In 1982, I appeared in the Harvard Lampoon's People magazine parody—in triplicate. I'm playing the Bother Brothers, who annoy people for a living. The caricature behind me is by future Simpsons writer Jeff Martin.

CHAPTER THREE

FUNNY FOR MONEY

It was April of my senior year and I had no postgraduation plans or career prospects. I thought that because I went to Harvard, God would provide. And they did. (I'm a polytheist.)

My break came when I got a call from Ted Mann, an editor at *National Lampoon.* In its heyday, *National Lampoon* magazine was the sole outlet for irreverent, adult humor in America; it was like *The Onion, The Daily Show,* and *SNL* all rolled into one. Ted said, "We've been reading your articles in the *Harvard Lampoon,* and we'd like to hire you."

"You read the *Harvard Lampoon*?" I asked, incredulous.

"We've been reading it for years," he replied. "We just never saw anything good before."

They hired my roommate and writing partner Al Jean as well. So a month after graduation, we moved to New York City, sharing a chic industrial loft in SoHo, over a hat factory. At *National Lampoon,* we made our own schedule, wrote what we wanted, and earned a cool $22,500 a year. That may not sound like much now, but back in 1981, it was still terrible.

Al and I distinguished ourselves early on with an article called "How to Write Dirty, by Justice Thurgood Marshall." This may seem like a non sequitur, but it was rooted in fact: Back in the eighties, the Supreme Court was forced to screen a lot of pornography in judging First Amendment cases. Some of the justices looked away from the porn, and some boycotted the screenings altogether. Justice Thurgood Marshall brought popcorn!

We wrote this silly, raunchy article, giving Thurgood way too many Supreme Court puns: "Hey, Felix Frankfurter—suck my wiener!" and "I told Harry Blackmun, 'I'm the real hairy black man around these parts.'" We published it thinking, with good reason, Thurgood would never see it. But if he did see it, he might actually like it!

Ten years later, when Thurgood Marshall passed away, his obituary was the top story in the *Los Angeles Times*. The first paragraph was about his being the first African American appointed to the Supreme Court. The second paragraph talked about his work as a lawyer in the landmark case *Brown v. Board of Education*. The very next paragraph said he was so offended by a particular *National Lampoon* article, he launched an FBI investigation into the writers. That's right: somewhere, I have a file.

Although we loved the *National Lampoon* job, Al and I were dreaming of bigger things. So after work, we'd moonlight on other projects—book proposals, TV pilots—hoping something would pay off. At one point we even wrote a screenplay for the rock star Meat Loaf. When we turned in the script to Mr. Loaf (that's what you call him), his secretary told us, "Come back next week and we'll give you five thousand dollars."

We came back the next week . . . and Mr. Loaf was gone. The office was abandoned. As I recall, they'd actually nailed boards up over the windows, in case I wanted my money . . . and was a zombie.

This was my first movie job.

My last movie job was in 2016. I sold an original screenplay to a very famous, Oscar-winning producer. He still owes me $250,000. The lesson here is, "You don't judge success by the amount of money you make. You judge it by the amount people are willing to screw you out of."

Ten months after we'd started at *National Lampoon*, Al and I got another call asking if we wanted to come to Hollywood and write jokes for a new comedy. It's a film you might have heard of. It was called *Airplane*.

II.

Airplane II: The Sequel. You may have seen it: it was a comedy so bad it actually won an award in France. (Esteem has risen for the film over the past few decades. Someone sent me a podcast recently where Quentin Tarantino raves about it, and the host keeps asking, "Are you sure you mean *Airplane II*?")

The call to work on the film came from its writer/director, Ken Finkleman. He had wanted our friends Tom Gammill and Max Pross, but they were busy, so they recommended us. (You might remember them from chapter 1: they turned down jobs on *The Simpsons* and recommended us for that. I owe my whole career to Tom and Max's bad judgment.) Finkleman called us on a Sunday night; Monday morning, we quit our *National Lampoon* jobs, ran out on our New York lease, and flew to Hollywood. Our landlady, I think with some bitterness, sent only one box of our possessions out to Los Angeles; it contained winter coats.

By Tuesday morning we were on the set of *Airplane II*. They were already shooting the film, and whenever a joke wasn't working, we were told to come up with something funnier—fast. We worked in a tiny wooden shed right on the stage, which was baking under hot studio lights. It was basically a sweatbox, the kind they send unruly convicts to in southern prison movies.

It was tough, high-pressure work—great training for our future jobs in TV—and we got lots of jokes in the final film. We also got to hang around with the all-star cast, which included many very nice people. And William Shatner.

Years later, we'd repay our debt to Ken Finkleman, getting him a staff job on *The Simpsons*. He spent some time in the writer's room, decided he didn't like it, and quit after two hours—a *Simpsons* record.

Where's Johnny?

After *Airplane II*, Al and I got another job, writing the script for a black comedy set in Vietnam, called *Cowards*. Al sent a copy of it to an actual Vietnam vet, who said, "I'd like to kill whoever wrote this."

That vet got his wish—the script killed our careers. The film never got made and we were finished in the film business. (The next movie job we had was writing *The Simpsons Movie*, twenty years later.)

It was 1984, and we were out of work in Los Angeles, a town where we knew no one. Al was applying to business schools and I was considering a career in alcoholism when we got a call from *The Tonight Show Starring Johnny Carson*. The head writer wanted to hire us pending an interview with Carson himself. When we stepped into Carson's office for the interview, we found it set up exactly like the *Tonight Show* set. With us on the couch and Johnny behind a desk, we chatted amiably for twelve minutes— the exact length of a *Tonight Show* segment. Carson made a joke, we laughed, and he sent us on our way. If he could have cut to an Alpo commercial, he would have.

The job was ours, and we were thrilled. But for Johnny, these were dark days: he was pushing sixty, was two decades into his show, and was going through his third divorce. He was so isolated from his writers that we read *National Enquirer* to find out what was going on in his life. One day the cover story was "Johnny's Ex Demands Five Thousand More a Week Alimony." Mickey Rose

Mural in Johnny Carson's hometown of Norfolk, Nebraska. It's a tribute to my writing the worst Carnac ever.

(cowriter of Woody Allen classics *Bananas* and *Take the Money and Run)* turned to another Carson writer and said, "That's funny. Between the two of us, we make five thousand a week."

The accountants must have noticed that, too—a few days later, both writers were fired.

The Tonight Show was a tough gig. Al and I were expected to write *sixty* jokes a day. Sixty jokes a day! What if you get writer's block? Well, if you work for a nightly show, you can't get writer's block. Why should you? Other professions don't have this luxury. A plumber doesn't come to your house and say, "I can't fix your toilet—I have plumber's block."

And an accountant never says, "I can't do your taxes, man. I have H&R Block."

AUDIENCE: Boo!

Where did they come from?

Every day, the five writers would each turn in sixty jokes to head writer Ray Siller. From those three hundred jokes he'd select the eighteen best. Of those eighteen, Carson would choose his dozen favorites. That's right: twelve jokes chosen from three hundred submitted—only 4 percent made the cut. Still, night after night, one out of every three jokes would bomb. It was the same during my years running *The Simpsons*: one out of three scripts bombed at the table reading.

No other business works like this. Campbell's can't say, "Great work, boys. Only one in three cans of our mushroom soup poisoned anyone!" At Samsung, do they say, "Congratulations, fellas. Only one in three of our phones exploded"? Actually . . .

One night Johnny was doing Carnac, the classic routine where he gives an answer followed by the question. A guy named Kevin Mulholland wrote what is considered the best Carnac ever:

ANSWER: Sis boom bah.

QUESTION: Describe the sound made by an exploding sheep.

I'm proud to say I wrote the worst Carnac ever:

ANSWER: Red Square.

QUESTION: What do you call that blotch on Gorbachev's head?

For you young people reading this, I'm not going to bother explaining who Gorbachev was, or what was on his head. Suffice it to say, the joke sucked. And yet somehow this gag made the final cut from the hundreds of Carnacs submitted. When Johnny performed it on the air that night, it met with a profound silence. The audience didn't dislike the joke—they had no idea it was one.

Six months later, Carson was doing Carnac again. Through some horrible clerical error, he chose the same joke: "Red Square."

Johnny read it . . . and it got a huge laugh! Same basic audience, same performer, same setting, same joke, but with a widely different response. I learned a valuable lesson that night: there's no science to comedy. (David Cohen, cocreator of *Futurama*, agrees with me on this. And he's an actual scientist.)

I will admit that there were two things that always got a laugh on *The Tonight Show*: when you called *Dynasty* star Joan Collins a bitch; and the word "McNuggets." Al and I wrote a joke, a perfect melding of these worlds: "Joan Collins has gotten a job working for McDonald's. She's endorsing their new product: Bitch McNuggets."

Now, that's not funny—I'm not even sure it's a joke. But Carson read it on the air and it got one of the longest laughs in the show's history.

How do I explain it? This was the eighties. All of America was on coke.

HERE'S JOANIE

I loved the weeks Joan Rivers hosted *The Tonight Show*. Every morning she would send us a list of topics for that night's monologue. For example:

WEDNESDAY

Cheerleaders

Roman Polanski

Beverly Hills High School

Madonna's wedding to Sean Penn

(For that last one we submitted the joke, "As part of her outfit, she's got something old, something new, something borrowed, and a blue movie she once starred in.")

One evening we heard that Joan's husband, Edgar Rosenberg, had a heart attack. We wondered if she would even do a show the next day. I mean, who'd expect her to? The next morning we got her list of topics:

THURSDAY

Edgar's heart attack

Edgar's lousy doctor

Edgar chasing nurses

Shopping for a funeral dress

The Sitcom Life

Two weeks after "Bitch McNuggets," Carson fired us for no apparent reason.

Two weeks after that, he offered us our jobs back, again for no apparent reason.

But Al and I had already moved into sitcoms, writing for *Sledge Hammer!,* a new parody series about a Dirty Harry–style cop. It was unique and irreverent, which are both crimes in network TV. ABC punished the show with one of the worst time slots in TV history: Friday night at nine, competing with *Dallas* and *Miami Vice,* the two biggest hits on the air. Still, *Sledge* hung on through two seasons and still has a nice cult following today. Since the show was shot on film without a studio audience, each script was like a little movie. The experience taught us to write cinematically, creating montages, quick cuts, and parodies of film tropes. We would put all these skills to use later on *The Simpsons.*

We jumped from *Sledge Hammer!* to *ALF,* a show about an alien hiding out with a family in suburbia. ALF ("Alien Life Form") was in fact a puppet voiced and operated by show creator Paul Fusco, one of the most talented men I ever worked with.

More importantly, the show was something new in our careers: a hit!

One thing we would take from *ALF* to *The Simpsons* was its suffusion of pop culture references. In the pilot for *ALF,* there was a line that every critic at the time singled out. When the family in the show is fighting, the father cries out, "Have we learned *nothing* from *The Cosby Show*?"

In 1987, this was a groundbreaking line! As Matt Groening once noted, people on TV never seem to watch TV. It's one reason our opening credits end with the Simpsons family piling onto the couch to stare at the television.

ALF's pop culture obsession reached a peak in an episode

where the alien dreams he's shipwrecked on *Gilligan's Island,* his favorite show. We assembled a majority of the cast as guest stars—sing it with me: Gilligan, the Skipper too, the professor, and Mary Ann. For a child of the sixties this was a dream come true—I got to write jokes for Gilligan. And hit on Mary Ann.

Because *ALF* was a show with a puppet, we knew kids would watch it, even if they didn't get the jokes. This freed us to write our scripts purely for an adult audience. One episode was an hour-long parody of *The Tonight Show,* which was on three hours past most kids' bedtimes. (I got to reuse some old Carnacs on that one!) This was a lesson we took to *The Simpsons*—don't write the show for kids; write it for the parents who will be watching with their kids.

ALF didn't pioneer this, by the way. *Mad* magazine never worried about what its audience might understand: it once did a cover story on *A Clockwork Orange,* an X-rated film that its core readers were too young to see. Years later, *The Simpsons* would do a Halloween show that parodied both *A Clockwork Orange* and *Eyes Wide Shut,* the Stanley Kubrick X-rated double feature. If your kids have seen these movies, I'm calling Child Protective Services.

I can trace this refusal to write down to your audience to *Rocky and Bullwinkle,* a show everyone at *The Simpsons* grew up watching. Apparently, the writers of that show (including Jim Brooks's old writing partner, Allan Burns) felt that the show's animation was so bad, the only way to save it was in the writing. As such, *Rocky and Bullwinkle* was a mix of silly puns and sophisticated Cold War satire; villain Boris Badenov was a nod to Boris Godunov, the sixteenth-century czar regent of Russia. Get it, kids? Of course not.

After a year on *ALF,* Al and I went off to work on *It's Garry Shandling's Show,* a show about a guy who knew he was on a show. Even the theme song was self-referential: "This is the theme to Garry's show / The opening theme to Garry's show . . ." The set was an exact replica of Shandling's actual living room.

People don't realize how much of *The Simpsons* came from *It's Garry Shandling's Show.* More than half our original writing staff—Sam Simon, Jay Kogen, Wally Wolodarsky, Al, and I— had done time on the series. The show was as unpredictable and self-aware as *The Simpsons* would be. The Shandling show also pioneered the use of the random guest star; for example, Jeff Goldblum and Tom Petty had recurring roles, as themselves, playing Garry's wacky neighbors. *The Simpsons* would do this later, but *Shandling* did it first.

Although we bounced from job to job and took whatever came our way, all these sitcoms taught us valuable lessons that we were about to use on *The Simpsons.*

SITCOMS

When a writer is considering whether to take a sitcom job, there are two basic criteria:

1. What are the hours like?

2. How long is the commute?

The hours on sitcoms vary wildly, from thirty-five hours a week to more than a hundred. And the workweek can be five, six, even seven days. "Eight Days a Week" is not just a Beatles song—it was the work schedule on *Arrested Development*. Their offices were next door to *The Simpsons*, and their writers seemed to work every single hour of every day. I used to imagine sweating workers in South African diamond mines saying, "This is bad, but it beats working for *Arrested Development*."

At *The Simpsons*, the work schedule has ranged from forty hours a week to more than eighty; it all depends on who's running the show. We currently have two writers' rooms running simultaneously, and they have completely different schedules: one gets out by six P.M.; the other room stays late but gets free dinner. (I opt for the free dinner!)

This being Los Angeles, the commute is just as important, because it doesn't matter that your day is short if you're spending three hours a day in rush hour traffic. (In L.A., rush hour is any hour of the day or night.)

It's Garry Shandling's Show was beloved by critics, but they didn't have to work there. The offices were way over in east L.A., and most nights we got out at two A.M.

By these standards, *ALF* was the best job I ever had—I was out at 7:30 every night, and home by 7:45.

You may be asking: *What about the quality of the show? Isn't that a consideration?*

Hey, that's funny. You could write sitcoms, too!

ACT TWO

A *Simpsons* plot, which begins at the very end of act 1, takes over in act 2. (*Simpsons* second acts often take up half the show.)

As this act 2 opens, I've left *It's Garry Shandling's Show* to work at *The Simpsons*. This section will take you behind the scenes of the show—you'll meet the writers, the actors, the animators, the producers. You'll learn step-by-step how we make the show. By the end of act 2, you're gonna be sick of the friggin' *Simpsons*.

Chapter Four

MEET THE WRITERS

Ninety-five percent of the work on *The Simpsons* isn't writing—it's rewriting. One person will write the script, but then it will be endlessly rewritten by a gang of writers: generally four to six people pitching jokes all day in one large room—the writers' room. (I briefly worked in a room with *twenty-seven* other writers. Absolutely nothing got done—people were afraid to pitch. If you made a joke and no one laughed, you had just bombed in front of a pretty decent-size crowd.)

A writers' room is a delicate thing—it's not enough to be funny; you also have to get along with everyone. One irritating or obstinate writer can bring the entire machinery of a show to a halt. I learned this long before *The Simpsons,* when I worked with a writer who was very talented but also an A-hole. (The *A* is for "ass.") Eventually, the boss called him in and said, "We love the work you're doing here, but everyone thinks you're an asshole. And we're going to have to fire you unless you can, you know, stop being an asshole."

The guy said, "Let me think about it."

He went home that night and returned the next morning. He said, "I discussed it with my wife and she agreed—I can't stop being an asshole."

The current *Simpsons* writing staff consists of twenty-three very funny non-assholes. People expect our writers' room to be a raucous madhouse, but it's not; it's a serious place of business. Every few years, a news program sends a camera crew to observe the *Simpsons* writers at work, and every time, the crew gets bored, then angry, and storms off without a second of usable footage. This is because our writers aren't clowns or performers—they're introspective, hardworking people who will spend two hours trying to think of a title for an Itchy and Scratchy cartoon. (Winner: "Of Mice and Manslaughter.")

These are not wild men—the *Simpsons* writers are mostly Family Guys who are American Dads (and one mom). None of us were Barts when we were kids. We were all Lisas, good, hardworking students with very few friends. And then one day we woke up, and we'd become balding, paunchy Homers. I'm not kidding when I say that every writer's favorite day is Friday. Why? That's free doughnut day.

In thirty years the most exciting thing that happened in our writers' room was when a writer got so frustrated because we couldn't get a joke we needed that he punched a cardboard box. His hand was torn and bloody, and the box was barely creased. That's our best story: a writer got in a fight with a cardboard box *and lost*.

Most of our current staff have been coming in, day in, day out, for more than a dozen years. It gives the place a small-town feel, like a Mayberry or a . . . Springfield; everyone knows each other's business. And just like in a small town, we're starved for novelty: when one of the writers shaved off his mustache, we talked about it for two years.

These cats are squares, daddio, but, man, are they funny. After thirty years at the show, I still walk into work intimidated by how sharp the other writers are. I rank myself as the eighth-funniest guy in the room, and I'm happy to make the top ten. I can't compete with Joel Cohen, a low-key guy from Calgary with the fastest mind alive. When we need a joke—say, a funny name for a nail salon—Joel will have spit out three pitches while the rest of us are still considering the problem. Then he'll make a joke about how lousy his first three ideas were, and pitch three more.

"Jesus, Joel," the other writers moan. Which is the best compliment you can get.

Our writers sprang up like genetic anomalies all over America. Only one is from a comedy background—Jay Kogen, whose father wrote for *The Carol Burnett Show* and, more impressive to us, *Mad* magazine. The rest of us are from small towns very much like Springfield: Utica, New York; New Canaan, Connecticut; Wilmington, North Carolina; Farmington Hills, Michigan. Showrunner Mike Scully is actually from Springfield—the one in Massachusetts.

How did they get to *The Simpsons*? Well, no writer has ever been hired without providing a writing sample first, no matter how impressive his résumé or how well we know him. He must submit a spec script—a sample episode of an existing TV show (like *The Big Bang Theory* or *Curb Your Enthusiasm*) that demonstrates that the writer can construct a clever, original story and knows how to write good dialogue in the style of known characters. I always tell aspiring writers, "Your spec is the last good writing you ever have to do." The strange thing, though, is that the spec script is never meant to actually be produced, and you almost never get a job at the show you wrote the script for. I broke into the industry with a *Golden Girls* script, which got me my next four jobs. But the *Golden Girls* didn't like it. I don't think anyone's ever been hired at *The Simpsons* off a *Simpsons* script.

In 1992 and '93, when I was running the show with Al Jean, I read eight hundred spec scripts a year—four hundred *Seinfeld*s, two hundred *Cheers,* a hundred *Murphy Brown*s, and assorted others. About seven hundred of these specs were good, but what I was looking for was great: I wanted a script that was funny from the first page to the last. I noticed how so many writers, in a hurry to finish, let the quality drop in the last few pages. I needed closers. This was the tedious process by which I found great writers, like Greg Daniels (creator of *The Office)* and Bill Oakley and Josh Weinstein, who three years later had my job running the show. In both cases, they had written pitch-perfect *Seinfeld* scripts. Greg's was set entirely in a single parking space and was so good that *Seinfeld* actually produced it. Bill and Josh's script had George Costanza accidentally swallowing a jagged piece of glass at a party; all the guests stay for hours, waiting to see if George "passes" the glass safely. It was cringe comedy at its very best.

I also rejected some very talented writers whose spec scripts weren't up to my standards. Some of these people would get hired later and do great work on the show: there's current *Simpsons* writers John Frink and Matt Selman and *Futurama* cocreator David Cohen, who may be the best *Simpsons* writer ever—he's the man behind the fans' all-time favorite episode, "The Itchy & Scratchy & Poochie Show."

Simpsons writers are scary smart, too. Ken Keeler has a Ph.D. in applied math. Jeff Westbrook has a Ph.D. in computer science. Bill Odenkirk[*] has a Ph.D. in inorganic chemistry, and helped cre-

---

[*] Bill Odenkirk is one of three *Simpsons* writers with famous funny brothers. Bill's brother is Bob Odenkirk of *Better Call Saul.* Writer Marc Wilmore's

ate 2,2′-Bis(2-indenyl) biphenyl—a ligand used to make organo-metallic complexes, dumbass. And then there's Dan Greaney, a graduate of Harvard Law School, where he and another student edited rival publications.

"Well, look at you now, Dan," I told him. "You've got a cool job writing for *The Simpsons*. What became of your rival?"

Dan replied, "He's Barack Obama."

Al Jean

When someone asks what's the secret of a great writing team, I say, "Find a brilliant partner and make him do all the work."

Al Jean was my writing partner for seventeen years. How brilliant is he? Here's an example. Once, during a writing session, I pitched a joke:

> At the nursing home, Grampa says, "I wanna watch TV!"
> Jasper snaps, "Who died and made you boss?"
>   Grampa says, "Fred," and points to an old man,
> lying on the ground, clearly dead and clutching the TV remote.

Everyone laughed, and it was about to go in the script when Al held up his hand. "I think we did it before." He told the writers' assistant to pull up a certain script—she has all six hundred episodes archived. Al didn't say, "Pull up the script where Grampa gets a girlfriend," or "Pull up 'The Old Man and the She.'" He

---

brother Larry hosted *The Nightly Show* on Comedy Central. David Stern's brother is actor Daniel Stern, the tall burglar who repeatedly gets the crap beat out of him in *Home Alone*.

said, "Pull up script 7F17"—the seventeenth script of our seventh season.

The writers' assistant put up 7F17 on the TV monitor.

"Go to page thirty," Al said. "Thirty-one. Thirty-two."

And there it was—the same joke, in a show we had produced twenty-three years ago.

"Let's keep pitching," Al said.

Al is my best friend and my best boss, and was the best man at my wedding. I met him the first week of college. He was passing by my dorm room and saw a rocking chair inside. "Would you mind if I rocked in your chair?" he asked.

It was an odd request, but he seemed harmless. He rocked for ten minutes and left.

Al Jean rocks! Not in the way the new iPhone X rocks (PRODUCT PLACEMENT—send me a crate of free phones, please). Al rocks in rocking chairs, in straight-back chairs . . . Legendary sitcom producer James Komack once said of him, "That kid rocks like an Orthodox Jew at prayer." I once gave Al a rocking chair for his birthday. He rocked it to pieces within a week. It's not an artistic quirk nor an autistic quirk—he just likes it.

When Al came to Harvard, he was taking pre-med courses, intending to be a doctor. But soon enough, I lured him into comedy with my tales of the *Harvard Lampoon*. I told him the parties were great (they were) and filled with beautiful women (they weren't). Thanks to my bad influence, Al Jean became one of the preeminent comedy writers in TV history. You're welcome.

Otherwise, he'd have become a doctor and cured cancer by now. And probably Alzheimer's. I'm sorry.

From 1981 to 1998, we wrote everything together, one line at a time. Of all the hours side by side, we fought maybe once a year, and it was never over our own material but about implementing some stupid note a network executive had given us.

If you want a good picture of how the team worked, see *Topsy-*

Turvy, Mike Leigh's great biopic of Gilbert and Sullivan. Gilbert (Al) is a tall, serious, hardworking perfectionist. Sullivan (me) is his shrimpy, merry, procrastinating partner.

After seeing the film, Al was stunned. "They even looked like us," he said.

Al is a great comedy writer, but he would have been great at whatever he devoted that massive throbbing brain to: farming, pharmacology, interpretive dance. But it could have all gone horribly wrong. Al read about another guy who had the exact same bio as his: a small-town kid from Michigan who came to Harvard at age sixteen to study math. It was Ted Kaczynski, the Unabomber.

Who knows? If Kaczynski had been just a little funnier, he might be running *The Simpsons* today. Or maybe *The Big Bang Theory.*

AL JEAN ON MIKE REISS

"I've known him for forty years and he's always an amazingly brilliant, funny guy. Morning, noon, and night. People would say, 'Does one of you write jokes and the other write setups? Does one of you do more structure and the other more dialogue?' Really, we'd just go line by line. We would start on a story and say, 'Okay, how do we start?' And one of us would say something, and if we both liked it, it would usually go in."

John Swartzwelder

John Swartzwelder, writer of nearly sixty *Simpsons* episodes, doesn't give interviews, go to parties, or do *Simpsons* DVD commentaries. As a result, he has taken on a mystique that combines

J. D. Salinger, Banksy, and Batman. John wasn't seeking this persona, but it amuses him deeply.

There's even an internet fan theory that John Swartzwelder doesn't exist—it's just a name we put on episodes that are group-written by the *Simpsons* staff.

Someone once called Swartzwelder "the Thomas Pynchon of the comedy world," which is oddly appropriate, because both these recluses have appeared multiple times on *The Simpsons*: Pynchon played himself in two episodes; Swartzwelder appears as a background character in many scenes (he closely resembles Wild Bill Hickok). In addition, for some reason, one Springfield park has a statue of Swartzwelder sitting on a horse, and for some reason, he is wearing a spiked German army helmet. (Swartzwelder loved using the phrase "for some reason" in his scripts. It justifies the unjustifiable, for some reason.)

I hate to demystify him, but he's a normal person, a strapping, friendly man who will chat endlessly about guy stuff like baseball and old westerns. His clothing and political affiliation are conservative. He smokes unapologetically. He reminds you of one of your father's friends.

But while John is (mostly) normal, his writing is not. He's responsible for a huge number of truly crazy *Simpsons* episodes, like the one where Bart gets an elephant; or where Homer becomes a henchman for a Bond villain; or where Marge . . . well, he never really liked writing for Marge. And he'd often "forget" to put Lisa in scripts. But he seemed to be able to effortlessly channel Homer. His secret, he said, was to write Homer as a big dog.

An example: In one episode, Homer is in prison. (Fun fact: after thirty seasons, every single member of the Simpsons family has been to prison, many of them twice!) Marge has baked him a cake with a file in it and delivers it to him; Homer wolfs it down, file and all. At this point, Swartzwelder proposed that a long pointy object begin to emerge in the back of Homer's pants.

We asked him, with some concern, "Just to be clear . . . you're saying that while Homer is talking to Marge, he's slowly shitting in his pants?"

Swartzwelder replied, in his Gary Cooper–like cadence, "Yessir, that's what I'm sayin'."

Not all the craziness was confined to his scripts. Swartzwelder would often make pronouncements like "The best exercise is to run ten feet as fast as you can and then stop short." Or "[*Bonanza* star] Lorne Greene invented rap music." Or "Abraham Lincoln was an asshole." He made these declarations with such confidence that he was sure everyone agreed with him.

One of the *Simpsons* writers, Jennifer Crittenden, left the show to work on *Seinfeld*. If a line was needed for Kramer, she would often pitch something Swartzwelder had said.

It always got rejected. "Too crazy for Kramer," the other writers would say.

John Swartzwelder is a normal guy. But he's crazier than Kramer.

Conan O'Brien

I've known Conan O'Brien since he was nineteen years old, and stardom hasn't changed him one bit. He was always an arrogant prick.

That's a joke—he's warm, modest, and the funniest man on earth.

I first heard about him when I was working in New York at *National Lampoon*. I got a call from a younger friend at the *Harvard Lampoon*, saying, "We just elected a guy on staff and he's like nothing we've ever seen."

(Left to right:) Charlie Brown's severed head, Conan, and me.

They said his name was Conan, so I asked to speak to him: "Conan, eh? Conan the Barbarian?" I wasn't being a jerk; I was being a *parody* of a jerk, which is still kind of jerky. "Where's your sword? Where's your broadax?"

Conan replied, "I don't have a broadax, but I like Al Brodax, producer of the *Popeye* cartoons." It was an insanely obscure reference, but he knew it and he knew I'd know it. I call it comedy telepathy. You probably call it geekiness. Shut up.

When Conan got out of college in 1985, I recommended him for his first TV job: HBO's sketch show *Not Necessarily the News.* He was then writing with future TV titan Greg Daniels. They were hired as a team, splitting scale, the lowest salary you can legally pay writers. It was the greatest bargain in TV history.

A decade later we hired Conan at *The Simpsons;* he was our first new writer since the show began in 1989. Al and I put him to work rewriting a script that had problems—the legendary, never-to-be-produced episode where the rock star Prince visits Springfield. Conan did such a good job that we had him fix another script. And then another. Finally John Swartzwelder told us, after witnessing Conan slaving away, "I saw the new guy working in his office. He looks like a dog being punished."

We finally brought Conan in to the writers' room, and he instantly took it over: He pitched great jokes. He entertained the staff. It was a nonstop show from ten in the morning till two at night. When he came to his first story meeting, he sold three ideas to the producers (including the classic monorail episode)—a record that stands to this day.

He left *The Simpsons* a quarter century ago to do his own talk show; he's hosted the White House Correspondents' Association Dinner twice and the Emmys three times. But he says people still ask him, "When are you going to write another *Simpsons*?"

Sooner or later, he'll come crawling back.

CONAN O'BRIEN ON WORK AT THE SIMPSONS

"I loved making Mike laugh. Of course, he was always trying to make me laugh, too. But I just remember it feeling aspirational to get Mike to laugh, because he has such a great one. Sometimes I wouldn't even say anything. I would just make odd noises to make Mike laugh, because when you're in the *Simpsons* writing room for fifteen hours subsisting on fried food, you just look for ways to make your comedy elders laugh.

"I remember they used to make me perform for them at *The Simpsons*. I was like their pet monkey in the room. I would do different things, a whole spectrum. The stupidest thing was I would fill my mouth with Coca-Cola and then would violently shake my body so I would look like I was having a wild fit, foaming at the mouth. I would really go for it. I remember their really enjoying that, and then applauding afterwards."

How Do We Make the Show?

It takes us nine months, from concept to finished product, to make a single episode of *The Simpsons*. Like that other nine-month process—pregnancy—it starts off fun, and ends up painful, messy, and expensive.

The procedure involves twenty-three steps—by contrast, performing a liver transplant takes only eight. So if you get bored reading about our process, feel free to bail out at any point. Just skip ahead to the end to see how you rank.

1. **THE PITCH:** Once or twice a year, the writers meet in a conference room to present their ideas to the executive

producers. The bosses kick each idea around, and if they approve it, they bang a gong. This is the only whimsical thing that happens in the whole process.

2. **THE SCRIPT:** The writer goes home for two weeks to write the script—it's about forty-five pages long.

3. **THE NOTES:** The showrunner annotates the script thoroughly, noting what must be changed.

4. **THE REWRITE:** Six to eight writers sit together with copies of the script, trying to address the notes. They all pitch jokes until something makes everyone laugh—that's the line that goes in. The writers' room is a democracy where you vote with laughter—like a kibbutz, only more Jewish.

5. **THE RE-REWRITE:** Once that roomful of writers has revised the script, it is handed off to a second writers' room for a final polish. And then a second final polish.

6. **THE TABLE READ:** The writers, the staff, and their guests—maybe sixty people in all—gather to hear the cast perform the script in a large room. (At least two cast members are not there, and read their parts on the world's tinniest speakerphone.) The writers mark their scripts, noting which jokes got a laugh from the audience and which didn't. They also get a sense of whether the storylines work and all the writing is true to character.

7. **YET ANOTHER REWRITE:** Armed with this info, the staff goes through another rewrite and another polish.

8. **THE RECORD:** The cast comes in a few days later to record their lines. They are directed by one of the writers, and perform four or five versions of each line.

9. **THE AUDIO EDIT:** The best take on each line is chosen, and a complete audio version of the episode is cut together—it runs about twenty minutes and plays like a radio show, complete with placeholder music and sound effects.

10. **THE DESIGN:** A writer works with the animators on designs for the episode—new characters, props, and costumes have to be drawn and approved. It's much more laborious than it sounds. For example, it's easy to write, "The Simpsons are at a costume party." But the designers have to determine who's at the party and what costume each attendee is wearing. In the early days, *everything* had to be designed. The first time we had rain on the show, we had to figure out: What does Bart wear in the rain? How about Lisa? Does Marge have an extra-long umbrella to cover her hair? What does *Simpsons* rain even look like—is it lines or drops? Is it yellow?

11. **STORYBOARDS:** Animators assemble a three-hundred-page black-and-white storyboard—basically a *loooooong* comic strip. It contains drawings of every key shot, action, and emotion in the script, with the dialogue pasted below. The showrunner, the script's writer, and particularly Matt Groening make detailed notes and fixes—this is the last step before any animation begins.

12. **THE ANIMATIC:** Two months after the table read, the writers and animators pack into a small room to watch the animatic: this is a roughly animated version of the storyboards, synced up to the edited audio track. It's like watching an episode of *The Simpsons* animated by cavemen on a tight budget.

13. **THE ANIMATIC REWRITE**: Based on reaction to the animated screening, the writers do another rewrite, fixing jokes that don't work, tossing out whole scenes and adding new ones. Up to a quarter of the script is changed at this point.

14. **ANIMATIC REVISIONS**: Actors come in to record new lines, new scenes are storyboarded, and a new audio track is assembled. Then the whole mess is ready to be shipped off to South Korea for full animation.

15. **FENG SHUI**: Jean Huang, a Los Angeles feng shui expert, examines the revised animatic to determine if it is in harmony with the series as a whole. She will then bless the show with incense and incantations.

16. **NOT REALLY**: Ignore step 15. We don't do that.

17. **ANIMATION**: Our team of Korean animators hand-draws twenty-four thousand cels to make one episode of *The Simpsons;* these days, color is added by computer, but for the first decade of the show, each cel had to be hand-painted. Backgrounds must also be designed and composited with the foreground animation. This process takes two months.

18. **COLOR SCREENING**: The writers and animators meet again in the screening room to see the finished animation and judge which scenes and jokes work. A joke from the first draft must get a laugh *three times* from the same group—at the table read, animatic, and color screening—to stay in the show.

19. **COLOR REWRITE**: A day is spent rewriting the color version—this is surgical work, since new animation is

costly. Typically, 10 percent of the script will be changed, re-recorded, and reanimated.

20.   **EDITING**: The revised color episode is edited for pacing. Then the showrunner picks the spots where music and sound effects should go.

21.   **SCORING**: Our composer devises an original score for the show—a single *Simpsons* episode may have as many musical cues as a feature-length film. The composer then records his score with a full orchestra.

22.   **MIXING**: In a daylong process, dialogue, music, and sound effects are combined into the final version of the show. Matt Groening and the producers will spend hours adjusting sound levels, making sure everything is as clear and funny as it can be.

23.   **AIR**: Four days after the mix, the show is aired. Then we rerun the living crap out of it.

It's that simple! It's taken nine months and eight full rewrites to bring a single episode to air. About 80 percent of the script has changed from the first draft—sometimes, not a single line remains from the original script. If a writer fights to preserve his original script, he'll probably get fired; there's no room in this process for ego.

Oh, and we have to do all this twenty-two times a year.

HOW MANY STEPS DID YOU READ BEFORE GIVING UP?

1–5: Haw-haw!

6–10: D'oh!

11–15: Underachiever and proud of it.

16–20: A true *Simpsons* fan.

21–23: Nerd.

Story Retreats

A story retreat is like New Year's Eve—it's how we kick off each season of *The Simpsons*. And like New Year's Eve, it was fun when we were young, but now it's something to be dreaded.

The procedure never changes: every writer comes in with a pitch for a new episode; then the rest of the staff, particularly James L. Brooks, riff on the idea until we decide we have enough for an episode. Brooks is almost supernaturally good at creating stories. You give him an idea, and he'll instantly spin out the whole episode, with jokes, plot twists, new characters, and a sweet and satisfying ending.

Al and I once pitched a germ of an idea: Marge takes an art class and churns out depressing Edvard Munch–like paintings; the family realizes she's secretly unhappy. From that nugget, Jim instantly spun out the plot of "Brush with Greatness," in which Marge is commissioned to paint Mr. Burns's portrait. Unable to find a way to make him sympathetic, she ultimately portrays him as twisted, frail, and nude. Jim told the story with the ease of someone recounting a TV show he saw the night before. He even laughed, surprised by his own jokes.

Occasionally, an idea is shot down, for being either too bland (the Simpsons visit Detroit) or too weird and arcane, such as the episode where Marge is kidnapped by Frenchmen seeking to restore the Bourbon monarchy. But just as often, a truly bizarre idea will get approved, such as an entire episode told by tattoos crawling over Homer's body. (I should note that this idea was approved, but never produced. Later, it wound up in *Moana*.)

Where do these ideas come from? From TV, magazines, movies, and our own lives. In one episode, Lisa drinks the water on an "It's a Small World"–type ride and begins hallucinating violently. We didn't make that up; it happened to our writer Kevin Curran. Of course, Lisa did this when she was eight years old. Kevin was thirty-two.

In another instance, one of our writers traveled to China in order to adopt a baby girl. We didn't say "That's great!" or "Congratulations!" We said, "Oh! We gotta use that on the show!" We wrote an episode where Patty and Selma go to China and adopt a baby girl.

The next year the same writer traveled to China to adopt another baby girl. And we said, "Dude. We did that episode already!"

So he went back to China and returned the baby.

Finally, from my own life came the Tale of the Clown Bed, a story that so tickled Matt Groening, he insisted we use it on the show. In 1992's "Lisa's First Word," Homer builds Bart a bed shaped like a clown's body, with a headboard painted to look like the clown's head. While the idea of a child sleeping on a clown's midriff every night is pretty weird, it's the headboard that made it awful: Homer has painted it with an unintentionally ghastly clown face. The finished bed scares the crap out of Bart, who sits up all night, quaking and chanting, "Can't sleep, clown'll eat me. Can't sleep, clown'll eat me." The clown bed was so memorable, it made a return appearance on the show twenty-two years later. It also pops up in two *Simpsons* video games and as a popular GIF.

My father built the original clown bed for my little brother, John, back in the sixties. The clown face Dad painted may have been even scarier than Homer's: the eyes were two soulless black pits; the nose was a weird pink color, with black flaring nostrils. It was so creepy, my mom insisted the head be removed; it wound up leering in the back of a closet, like a scene from the

Bart's horrifying clown bed is based on one my father built.

movie *It*. My brother spent the next several years sleeping in a headless clown.

In the early days, story pitches were a couple of minutes long: a premise, a few sample jokes, and a conclusion. Over time, these pitches have swelled to become detailed fifteen-minute presentations. Many writers even bring in visual aids; one woman brought musical accompaniment. Al Jean once circumvented the whole process—he plopped a finished script on the table and said, "Here's my pitch."

My brother John's re-creation of the clown bed head he was forced to sleep under.

As the pitches become more elaborate, the settings in which we pitch become more spartan. Nowadays we do these sessions in a conference room on the Fox lot. But in the early days of the show, we'd hold them in a luxury hotel suite, often with an ocean view. (This is why we called these story conferences "retreats.") At the end of the day, if one of the writers had a girlfriend (a rare occurrence back then), he'd get to stay in the suite for the night.

The greatest part of any retreat was getting a story approved—this was celebrated by banging a huge ceremonial gong. We used to get one from the studio prop department, until Fox began asking if gong rental was a necessary expense (bean counters!). After that, we started using a small gong someone stole from a Chinese restaurant; when that got stolen from us, we would bang the lid on an ice bucket. Now we just rap a fist on a tabletop.

I'm often asked if I'm afraid the show will run out of ideas. It's never a concern of mine. It helps having a big writing staff: twenty-three writers have to produce twenty-two stories a year; which means each writer needs to have only one good idea a year. If my math is correct it also means that one guy doesn't have to do squat.

I am that guy.

Jokes That Never Quite Made It

The Simpsons has so many running jokes—the location of Springfield, Bart's prank calls, Burns's hound-releasing, Lenny getting severe eye damage—but there are some that haven't caught the public's fancy. Even our most obsessive fans haven't picked up on these. Now they have something new to obsess about:

🍺 **HOMER IS AN EXPERT ON THE SUPREME COURT:** We've mentioned this a couple of times—for some reason, Homer knows the names of all our chief justices.

🍺 **SKINNER WEARS A TOUPEE**: He does! We just never show it or mention it. We put the jokes in, but they always get cut. The lone vestige is one of Bart's chalkboard gags: "THE PRINCIPAL'S TOUPEE IS NOT A FRISBEE."

🍺 **MARGE'S FATHER'S DEATH**: We thought that every time we mentioned Marge's father's death, there would be a different funny cause: he got drunk and fell off a roller coaster, he was eaten by a bear at the circus . . . None of these jokes was funny enough to make the final cut of the show. Finally, in season 27, we said he died of lung cancer. Not really funny.

Sometimes I can't fathom why jokes don't make it into the script. For example, once, we wanted Marge to be reading a news magazine about tar. (It's a long story.) We needed a name for the magazine, and I pitched *Tar Nation* (as in "What in tarnation?!"). Everyone seemed happy, except Al.

"Nah," he said, rejecting it.

"Nah?" echoed writer George Meyer, incredulous. But I wasn't mad—someday, somewhere, someone will need a name for a weekly tar magazine, and I've got one.

Another bit you never saw was a long scene with Lenny and Carl discussing Ted Danson's forgotten sitcom *Becker* as if it were as great as *Star Trek*. They knew every bit of trivia about the show, called themselves "Beckies," and were planning to attend a big *Becker* convention that weekend.

The writers' room loved it, but you probably had to be there. The showrunner at the time walked in and cut it instantly. He also cut another bit we liked—a character named Gravy Wallace who loved gravy. That was it—Gravy Wallace loved gravy. Maybe the showrunner was right and it was stupid. But maybe Gravy could've been the next Disco Stu.

There's Always a Joke

I'm not a spiritual man. I don't believe in ghosts or astrology or reincarnation. And if the Dalai Lama is so godlike, why does he need glasses? Although I'm Jewish, I'd happily eat a ham sandwich. With mayo. In a synagogue. On Yom Kippur.

I have only one supernatural belief: No matter what the setup, there's always a perfect joke for it. It may not be a great joke, but it's always *the right joke* for the moment: it's there in the universe, waiting to be discovered.

I came to this conclusion after we spent three hours trying to come up with a certain joke on *The Simpsons*. Here's the setup: Homer enters Lisa in the Little Miss Springfield pageant, and she wins. She becomes an outspoken activist (we based her on Jane Fonda), and pageant officials fear she's turning into a liability. They scan Homer's entry form, looking for a mistake so they can disqualify Lisa, and they find . . . what?

We pitched longer on this joke than any I can remember. Some suggestions made Homer look too stupid, others too lazy; worst of all, none of them were funny. We were stumped. We knew Homer's mistake had to be an innocent one, but one so undeniable that it could get Lisa eliminated—this was the resolution of the whole episode.

By one in the morning, we were exhausted, frustrated, and ready to settle for a lame joke . . . or no joke at all. That's when a writer named Frank spoke up. Frank wrote great scripts, but he rarely spoke—he was a Buddha-like man who would plop himself into a chair first thing every morning, shut his eyes, and go silent. He was either meditating, sleeping, or dead. In any case, we'd whisper around Frank all day, not wanting to disturb him. But on this particular session, just when we were about to give up, Frank opened his eyes and said, "In the space marked 'Do not write in this box,' Homer wrote 'OK.'"

Perfect.

(Weeks later, Frank would pitch another great joke. It was a Troy McClure driver's ed film called *Alice's Adventures Through the Windshield Glass*. Then he went back to sleep.)

Since the Frank incident I've always believed that the perfect joke is out there if you're willing to spend the time searching for it. And sometimes you have to think outside the box. (Although that's a cliché: anyone who says "think outside the box" isn't thinking outside the box.) For one script, we needed a funny name for a family restaurant franchise. Some of us pitched parodies of TGI Fridays: Too Bad It's Mondays, Thank Allah It's Ramadan, etc. Other pitches burlesqued cutesy names like the Old Spaghetti Factory: the Corndog Conglomerate, the Lasagna Limited Holding Corporation. The problem with making jokes from a formula is that they sound ... formulaic. Then George Meyer piped in with his restaurant name: The Texas Cheesecake Depository. I have no idea where that joke came from, but I know where it went: into the script immediately, into syndication eternally.

(George pitched another great restaurant joke, but we never found a spot for it: in a diner serving chicken wings and potato skins hung a sign reading, THANK YOU FOR EATING OUR GARBAGE.)

I can only think of one time where the *Simpsons* writers settled for a joke they knew was subpar. We were working on 1992's "Three Men and a Comic Book," the episode that introduced Comic Book Guy. The character seemed so marginal, we didn't even bother to name him. It was past midnight and we were getting ready to leave, when one writer asked, "Shouldn't we name his store?" We pitched for a while and finally settled on "The Android's Dungeon and Baseball Card Shop." This is what writers call a "wacky stack," a string of funny words that they hope will somehow become a joke (see the glossary). I figured it was good enough, since we'd only see this comic-book store this one time.

Since then, we've shown this shop, and it's not-quite-funny sign, in dozens of episodes. I'm embarrassed every time. (They've even built a life-size replica of the store at Universal Studios Hollywood—I hate it.)

It reminds me of a legendary exchange between two sitcom writers: one of them pitched a joke and the other said, "I don't know. It's *too* easy, it's *too* pat—"

"It's *two* in the morning," said the first writer. "Put it in."

My faith in the existence of the perfect joke guided my writing on *Ice Age: Dawn of the Dinosaurs*. In the film, Sid the sloth finds three dinosaur eggs, and I decided he should give each one a name.

The first egg was easy: Egbert. I've never met anyone with this name—it may exist only as a gift to comedy writers.

The second egg was tougher. I racked my brain thinking of egg-related words: poultry, poached, omelet, shell . . . That's it! The second egg would be Shelly.

But what about the third? Did it even exist? I knew from experience it was out there somewhere.

Days later, I hit on the third name for an egg.

Yoko.

JUDD APATOW ON PITCHING

"I would sometimes see Mike and Al sit on a joke *for an hour*. If they didn't like the jokes, there were times they would just sit there pitching. Or in silence. For *so long*. Until they decided they had a strong enough joke. Watching them try to figure out what was strong and what wasn't was how I learned to be a comedy writer. Just seeing what jokes Mike and Al rejected teaches you a lot."

DAN CASTELLANETA ON PITCHING

"Something I've learned from Mike: *Keep pitching, no matter what!* Don't worry if they don't use your best stuff; there's more to come. It's nothing to Mike not to have something he pitched put in; he just comes up with another thing right after. Don't be so precious about coming up with something funny if someone turns it down, because there's always more."

Research

Sam Simon decreed when we were starting the series, "If you hear a fact on *The Simpsons,* it has to be true." Whether the characters are speaking Albanian or discussing the finer points of Hindu theology, the show gets it right. When the Simpson family visits another country, which they do every year, we bury ourselves in travel books. Unlike in college, the *Simpsons* writers do their homework.

During the Simpsons' trip to London, we had a policeman blow his whistle and no sound came out. The constable then uttered the preposterous line, "Oh that's right. I sent my whistle-ball out to be polished." On the script, writer Ian Maxtone-Graham scrawled the note *English police whistles don't have balls.* Who knows these things?

Of course, it's easy to Google facts now, but *The Simpsons* predates the internet. Luckily, the early *Simpsons* writers, between them, contained *all of human knowledge.* Some guys knew a lot about sports, others history, entertainment, science, potent potables, and potpourri. If there was something none of us knew, we'd consult a fat one-volume encyclopedia that sat on our table in the writers' room.

In a 1993 show, we had Apu state, "I can recite pi to forty thousand places. The last digit is—"

We didn't know. We could have guessed, and had a 10 percent chance of being right. Instead, we called Caltech. A few days later, they sent us a giant dot-matrix printout of pi to one million places. In case you're wondering, the forty-thousandth digit of pi is 1, which worked well for the joke. Thanks, God.

When simply calling up to fact-check wasn't enough, we did what any seasoned journalist or first grader would do: we took a field trip. Representatives from the nuclear power industry didn't like how it was depicted on our show (babies!), so they invited some of our staff to tour one of their plants. When Sam Simon returned that day, he said, "It was so much worse than we ever imagined!" His one takeaway from the nuclear power plant tour? "There's a candy machine every ten feet!" We faithfully worked this detail into the show.

Tales of Censorship

In 1990, Fox censors told us we could now use the word "ass" on TV. As a comedy writer, I "felt like some watcher of the skies, when a new planet swims into his ken" (Keats). Or, more baseline, how a drug addict felt when crack was invented. "Ass" was my crack.

We still couldn't use "ass" any way we pleased. In one script, we had the phrase "up his ass"; Fox censors asked us to change it to "in his ass." That seemed worse, but we did as they asked. In the next week's script, we wrote the phrase "in his ass." They made us change it to "up his ass"! Now, in hindsight (*wink wink*), why on a cartoon show did we need to say "up his ass" two weeks in a row? In fifty years of *Looney Tunes*, Elmer Fudd never said,

"I'm gonna catch that wascally wabbit and shove this gun *wight up his ass!*"

Fox Broadcast Standards (there's an oxymoron!) had one other restriction: we could use only one "ass" per episode. This became a problem when, in the third-season episode "Homer Defined," we wrote *two* great ass jokes. One had Bart, defending his character, saying, "Bad influence, my ass!" The other had Mr. Burns saying, in the case of nuclear meltdown, to "Kiss your ass goodbye." We could use only one—but which? This was our writers' *Sophie's Choice* moment. In the end, we put it to a vote, and Mr. Burns won. However, in the first rerun of the episode, Bart was the one who got to say "ass." If only America's democracy were this fair.

A few months later, Fox debuted a new series called *Bobcat's Big Ass Show,* in which the host Bobcat Goldthwait said "ass" virtually nonstop during the show. In fact, the phrase "Big Ass" was emblazoned on a giant sign behind him in every shot.

We haven't had many run-ins with the network over cursing—Fox's rules are fairly loose, and the *Simpsons* writers try to be accommodating. When we got the censor note, *Please change Bart's line "Bastard bastard bastard bastard,"* we didn't put up much resistance.

We will fight if we think the joke is really good and the network's objection is unreasonable. In "Homer Loves Flanders," Homer is chasing Ned's car, so Maude urges Ned to drive faster. He replies, "I can't—it's a Geo!" Fox hated the line—it could lose them a rich sponsor—but showrunner David Mirkin kept it in.

In another Mirkin show, "You Only Move Twice," he featured a James Bond–type character who introduces himself as . . . James Bond. Fox said he couldn't do that, so David changed the character's name in the script to James Bont.

And, just as easily, he had the actor record the line as "James Bond."

No discussion of censorship would be complete without mentioning the F-word: Fox. In theory, *The Simpsons* is liberal to the point of anarchy, and Fox is conservative to a point approaching fascism. People always ask, why do they let us get away with it?

First off, *The Simpsons* came to Fox before there was a Fox News Channel. At the time, Fox's reputation was daring and sexy. It was a perfect place for a show that could never have survived on any of the big three networks. Fox gave us immense freedom, and still does—they almost never question our content.

Why? Money. The people behind Fox are capitalists, and we bring in a lot of capital—$5 billion, by one estimate. (But no profit—I own 1 percent of *The Simpsons*' profit, and to date I've never gotten a penny. Every fiscal quarter, Fox sends me a statement that reads, *We've grossed five billion dollars, but our costs are five billion and eight dollars. You owe us eight cents.* I am living proof that not all Jews have business savvy.)

The other reason Fox gives us free rein is . . . they like us! They enjoy the show. Fox founder Rupert Murdoch has appeared on the series several times, including once as a convict. (His son James is an alum of the *Harvard Lampoon*.) And sometimes doing a funny show excuses everything. Media watchdog Parents Television Council has found offensive material in every show from *Family Guy* to *Flipper*. But they've never criticized *The Simpsons*. Why? Their founder, Brent Bozell, likes the show!

We once made vicious fun of Fox News in one episode (several episodes, actually, but one in particular). Soon a rumor went around that Fox News was suing *The Simpsons*. This was crazy, of course—it would be Rupert Murdoch suing himself. If he won the suit, he'd have to move money from his left pocket to his right.

The truth is, the day after that episode aired, we did get a call from Fox News.

They said, "Do it again!"

A Tale of Two Jokes

Two of the most famous *Simpsons* punchlines in history are "cheese-eating surrender monkeys" and "President Trump." In each case, they are random collections of words that make no sense at all.

The first appeared in the 1995 episode "'Round Springfield." Due to budget cuts at Springfield Elementary, Groundskeeper Willie is asked to teach French class. He enters with the line "*Bonjour,* ya cheese-eating surrender monkeys." Four years later, the line appeared in the *National Review* in Jonah Goldberg's article "Top Ten Reasons to Hate the French"—thus stealing Letterman's format and *The Simpsons*' joke. Later, he reused the line to criticize the French for not joining the U.S. in the Iraq War. From there, the British newspapers picked up on the phrase: it was quoted in the *Daily Mail* and the *Telegraph;* the *Times* of London said it was so overused as to become "a journalistic cliché." "Cheese-eating surrender monkeys" eventually made it into the *Oxford Dictionary of Modern Quotations.* England gave us Shakespeare, we gave them this.

The irony here is that all these esteemed Brits are quoting the hate speech of an alcoholic janitor on a cartoon show, and that it became popular because the French refused to join us in a trillion-dollar unwinnable war based on bogus intel . . . *and* because the French have the greatest victory rate of any army in world history. And what's so bad about eating cheese anyway?

When the line first was making news, Al Jean and I, who produced "'Round Springfield," could not recall which writer came up with it. Finally Ken Keeler took the credit, calling it his "greatest contribution to the show." He can have it.

The second big joke came from the episode "Bart to the Future," in which Lisa Simpson becomes "America's first straight female president." In this futuristic episode Lisa says, "We've inherited quite a budget crunch from President Trump." An impressive call, especially since we made it in 2000, sixteen years before Trump was elected. Virtually every news outlet mentioned the joke, but none of our writers can recall who pitched it. Or maybe nobody wants the blame.

One thing to remember about this prediction: "President Trump" was the *punchline* to the setup, "What's the dumbest thing we could imagine America doing?" When the news of the world becomes jokes on *The Simpsons,* that's satire. But when jokes on *The Simpsons* become the news of the world—well, that's just fucked up. The upside is that *The Simpsons* thrives on human stupidity—the dumber people get, the better our show is. And so, on November 8, 2016, President Trump was elected; on November 9, *The Simpsons* was picked up for two more seasons. President Trump has been good for business—my business!

Topicality

The biggest misconception people have about *The Simpsons* is that it's a topical show, ripped from today's headlines. Actually, it takes us nearly a year to produce a single episode, so we are, in fact, the least timely show on television.

Very often, this long lead time gets us into trouble. Eartha Kitt played herself in one episode, and by the time the show aired, she was dead. This Catwoman's appearance was . . . purr-plexing.

In another episode, Mr. Burns had the line "Well, I'm no young matinee idol like Rex Harrison." Two days before the show aired, Rex Harrison dropped dead. No one saw it coming—the man was only ninety-eight years old. We couldn't get Harry Shearer to come in and replace the line, so we took scissors and tape—this was the analog era—and recut the audio, changing it from Rex

Harrison to Redd Foxx, the star of *Sanford and Son*. The line now went, "Well, I'm no young matinee idol like Rrrreddddd Foooooxxxxx." It didn't look good, it didn't make sense, but at least we were spared an embarrassing situation.

The morning that show aired, Redd Foxx dropped dead. And it reminded me of something my grandfather told me as a little boy. He said, "Michael, God hates you."

> (FULL DISCLOSURE: I've been telling that story for years— and believing it. But I recently watched that episode again, and saw that we never changed the Rex Harrison line. And Rex Harrison was only eighty-two when he died. And Redd Foxx died sixteen months after that episode aired. Otherwise, I stand by my story.)

The biggest problem with topical jokes is they don't age well. One episode ended with Selma singing "(You Make Me Feel Like) A Natural Woman" to her pet iguana Jub-Jub. (That name was coined by Conan O'Brien.) This was a parody of a scene on the sitcom *Murphy Brown* that was considered unforgettable—until everyone forgot it. And in *The Simpsons Movie,* the family escapes from the dome in a shot-for-shot homage to the ending of the show *Prison Break*. Remember that? Neither do I.

I can think of only two times we tied *Simpsons* episodes to current events. The first was a 1996 Halloween segment where aliens Kang and Kodos take over the bodies of presidential candidates Bill Clinton and Bob Dole. During the nine months of production I worried that if something happened to either candidate—illness, resignation, assassination—before the show aired, it would ruin the episode. (It would be bad for America, too, but that wasn't my top concern.) Luckily, both candidates survived to Halloween, and later Election Day.

Two decades later we did an episode where the Simpson family visits Cuba, and it featured many scenes involving Fidel Castro.

If the ninety-year-old dictator died before the show aired, we'd be sunk—he was in too many scenes to cut. This put me in the awkward position of praying for the continued good health of an aging despot. With admirable stamina, Castro hung on until the episode aired, and passed away twelve days later. What a trouper!

The one place where we can do topical humor is in Bart's chalkboard jokes, which can be inserted into the show just days before it airs. One night we inserted a (fake) spoiler about the final episode of *Lost,* which happened to be airing against us. It read: "END OF LOST: IT WAS ALL THE DOG'S DREAM."

And after Donald Trump became president—as we'd predicted—Bart wrote on the blackboard: "BEING RIGHT SUCKS."

DAN CASTELLANETA ON ELECTION DAY

"There was one time, after the election, and everybody was basically stressed out and dismayed about Trump, and they were going on and on about it. Mike was just sitting there quietly listening and finally goes, 'Boy, I'm starting to feel really bad about voting for the guy.'"

The Joke I'm Proudest Of

My favorite joke I ever wrote for *The Simpsons* was a Troy McClure movie title: *P is for Psycho.* (I repeated that joke at a talk in Arkansas and everyone in the audience said, "No, it ain't.")

But let me tell you about the joke I'm proudest of.

One night Homer is watching TV, and an ad on it says, "Warning: Beer can cause liver damage, kidney failure, and cancer of the rectum."

And Homer says, "Mmmm . . . beer."

I wrote that joke, but it's not the one I'm proudest of.

The next day, Budweiser called and said, "Stop picking on beer!"

I said, "Come on—it was just one joke!"

And they said, "No, last week, Homer went to the Duff Brewery, and one of the bottles had Hitler's head in it."

And I wrote that joke, too, but it's still not the one I'm proudest of.

Budweiser was getting increasingly upset. They said, "We'll have you know that the president of our company, August Busch Jr., was considered a very big hero in World War Two!"

And I said, "By the Nazis?"

That's the joke I'm proudest of.

What's It Like?

A question I get all the time—mostly from my partner on this book , Matt Klickstein—is "What is it like?" What's it like writing for a classic TV show, one praised by critics, taught in colleges, quoted by clergymen, and beloved by fans in seventy-one countries? What's that like?

It's okay.

I'm not being blasé. Although I've devoted half my life to the show, if I'd never been born or had been hit by a bus or gone to Yale (something horrible like that), the show would be exactly as good. *The Simpsons* is a giant operation, with dozens of brilliant writers and hundreds of talented animators. It's been a huge part of my life, but I've been a small part of it. I'm like a guy who helped build the Great Pyramid of Giza: I can point with pride to three or four blocks that I dragged into place, but if it weren't me, it would be some other Hebrew slave.

I'll admit, *The Simpsons* has brought me a little fame. I get recognized at least once a month by the show's fans; some of them know me by my voice, which they've heard on *Simpsons* DVD

I get recognized about once a month . . . although usually people think I'm *House* star Peter Jacobson.

commentaries. I've even become a thinly veiled character in two novels; in one, I became "Ethan the ugly animation writer." And in 2014, when I was five days into hiking up Mount Kilimanjaro and had reached twelve thousand feet, I heard another hiker call out, "Hey, are you Mike Reiss?" It was a *Simpsons* superfan from Brooklyn. Though the air was very thin, I used the last of my oxygen answering this guy's questions about John Swartzwelder.

Still, it's impossible to get a big ego working at *The Simpsons,* because you're surrounded by old friends, wise guys, and professional cynics, all of whom will call you out on it. In three decades, I've seen only one writer get a swelled head. He came back from a vacation and told us, "Someone asked me to make a joke. I told them: I make America laugh three hundred and sixty days a year; don't I deserve five days to myself?"

The line was so ludicrous, we had Krusty say it in an episode. It's one of the few jokes that writer ever got on the show.

I won't lie—in 1990, at the height of Simpsonsmania, it was impossible not to get excited. *Simpsons* T-shirts were everywhere. Bootleg *Simpsons* T-shirts were even more widespread: black Bart; Mexican Bart; Bart smoking a joint; Bart stuck in a woman's ass ("Crack Kills"). Fox hired bootleg police (that's a thing), who impounded millions of illegal T-shirts. There was talk of donating them to Ethiopia, but Fox decided it might look bad—a nation of starving people all wearing Bart T-shirts. The bootlegs were destroyed.

Back in those heady days, a store opened in my neighborhood called Simpsons Forever: Nothing but Simpsons Merchandise. A few months later, the store widened its inventory and changed its name to Simpsons, Etc. And then Toon Fever. Within a year, it was called Out of Business.

These days, the best part of working for *The Simpsons* is that people know what it is—you don't have to explain it. These are the reactions I've had when I told people about my other writing jobs:

  🍺 *ALF*: "Is that the show with the talking dog?"

  🍺 *It's Garry Shandling's Show*: "Oh, I don't like him."

  🍺 *Sledge Hammer!*: "The Peter Gabriel song?"

  ME: "Yes, I work for the Peter Gabriel song. I'm Peter Gabriel."

So isn't it great working for something that's a part of American culture?

Meh.

A Day at *The Simpsons*: A Writer's Diary

April 3, 2017, was my 1,644th day writing for *The Simpsons*. To show you what it's like working there, I kept a log—this is exactly what happened that day. It was pretty much like the other 1,643 days I'd spent writing for the show:

10:00 A.M.: Work officially starts. I show up right on time.

10:14: No one's here. I do a crossword.

10:25: Still alone. I'm getting scared. Is it Saturday?

10:30: The boss shows up. One by one, the other writers drift in.

10:40: We start work on a script where Professor Frink gives everyone in town an IQ test. This is the fifth rewrite of the script.

10:45–11:12: We work on a joke for Ralph Wiggum. We don't get one.

11:13: We talk about the president.

11:20: We order lunch.

11:25: We talk about Paul Erdos, the Hungarian mathe-matician, for some reason.

11:30–12:28: We get back to work and write five jokes. We're on a real roll—nothing can stop us. Then the lunch bell rings.

12:29–2:10: Lunch hour! (One hour, forty-one minutes.)

2:11–3:05: More jokes written.

3:06: Two of our smartest writers, Jeff Westbrook and Dan Greaney, get into a heated debate about global trade. I check my email.

3:19–3:26: Awkward silence.

3:35: We go online to see a map of what the world would look like if the ice caps completely melted. It's not as bad as we thought.

3:56–4:12: We make good progress on the script.

4:13–5:02: We get stuck on a line for Rupert Murdoch.

5:03: I pitch the line that goes in the script: "If you're watching this show, I'm getting richer."

5:05: We place dinner orders.

5:06–5:40: We get stuck on the last line of the script: Homer is writing a love letter to Marge.

5:41: Jeff Westbrook pitches, "You're as beautiful as your sisters are hideous." It's good! We've finished the rewrite!

5:42: The boss decides to do a sixth rewrite of the script.

6:18: I get a joke in the script. It replaces a joke I wrote last week.

6:46: Dinner arrives. It's inedible. I eat it.

6:55–7:20: We can't think of a line for Mr. Burns to say to the ghost of Orson Welles. What the hell are we writing?

7:21–7:50: We work on an Apu doughnut joke. I pitch, "If the sprinkles are moving, don't eat them." The boss decides to cut the whole scene.

7:51: We need another Ralph line—it's the last joke of the day.

8:12: Dan Greaney pitches, "I shooted Daddy." The boss laughs and tells everyone to go home. We'll start our seventh rewrite in the morning.

BURNING QUESTION

Simpsons songs: Who writes them, how are they written, and why are there so goddamn many?

Good burning questions.

The show's writers do the lyrics—they're just little poems, and often our songs are parodies written to existing melodies. Then the series's composer (Alf Clausen for twenty-eight great seasons) writes original music for the songs, thereby covering our (musical) tracks.

Writer Jeff Martin wrote the words _and_ music for our musical parody of _A Streetcar Named Desire_. (Jeff's also a talented cartoonist, pianist, singer, and juggler. And, he's tall and good-looking. He's one of my best friends and I hate him.)

One reason we like using songs is that they fill up the show: our job as creative artists is to shovel jokes into a twenty-two-minute ditch each week. While any joke on _The Simpsons_ might be rewritten five or six times, songs rarely change and almost never get cut. One exception: "We Love to Smoke," a Patty and Selma number.

It was a funny take-off of *Mary Poppins*'s "I Love to Laugh," but hearing Patty and Selma rasp and cough out a song was pretty grating. (You can hear the audio for "We Love to Smoke" on YouTube. You'd cut the song, too.)

It's an ongoing debate at the show whether the public even likes these musical numbers. Personally, I loved all the original songs on *Monty Python's Flying Circus;* however, I generally tune out when I see one on *SNL*. In the end, songs are probably like jokes: they're good when they're good. Even better, you can make extra cash on them. I earn a couple of grand a year on songwriting royalties for "Spider-Pig," and I'm one of eleven credited writers on the song. I wasn't even in the room when it was written.

CHAPTER FIVE

MEET THE SHOWRUNNERS

Writing for *The Simpsons* is genuinely fun; running the show is like crawling nude over broken glass in hell. No one ever asks to be showrunner—the title is generally thrust upon some talented, hardworking sucker. Al Jean has been running the show for the past twenty years, and no one's ever tried to unseat him, because being showrunner on *The Simpsons* is like being mayor of Detroit: great title, crummy job.

In 1991, *The Simpsons* was going into its third season, and was a blockbuster, game-changing hit. Sam Simon, who'd been running the show, had moved on to develop new sitcoms. Al Jean and I, still in our twenties, were put in charge of the show with a mandate: Don't Screw It Up. And we had so many opportunities to screw it up! Our duties included supervising the writing, directing the voice actors, going over storyboards, approving character designs, editing voice tracks and final animation, and determining spots for music and sound effects. We were trained in absolutely none of this.

The pressure on us was immense; we were learning as we went along, working one hundred hours a week, fifty-one weeks a year (thank God for Christmas week!). Al and I would edit the show's audio track from eight to ten each morning, run the writers' room from ten A.M. till eight P.M. (where the writers bitched about *their own* hours), then go back to editing till two in the morning.

Once, nearing my breaking point, I took an emergency day off. At midnight, I gave my last note to the production team, saying that a background character should look like *Hollywood Squares* star Wally Cox. Then I left, asking not to be disturbed under any circumstances for the next twenty-four hours. The phone rang at seven the following morning: "Do you want Wally Cox before he had a mustache or after?" Arrghh!

We never missed a day, even when Al had pneumonia. I said something that made him laugh, but the laugh soon turned to a coughing fit, and he crumpled to the floor and passed out.

Oh no, I've killed Al, I thought. *I can't do this show alone.*

A minute later, Al came to, climbed back into his chair, and said, "Let's keep going."

Another time, I came to work with the flu. I sent a production assistant out to get me cough drops. The next day, I got an angry call from our budget guy: "What's this eighty-five cents you're billing to the show?" I'm not making this up—the budget guy was sick, too: he had six weeks to live, and he was fighting me over eighty-five cents.

"Pal," I said, "this is not a good use of either of our time."

At the end of season 4, I left to take my Christmas break. I picked up a year-end magazine that declared "the writing on *The Simpsons* has gone downhill." That critique ruined my holiday. I obsessed about what I could have been doing wrong. Twenty years later, that same magazine declared season 4 "the greatest season of the greatest show in history." Thanks.

During my two years running *The Simpsons,* I gained seventy pounds—I was working sixteen-hour days, living on take-out meals and junk food, never having the time or energy to exercise. When I finally got to a doctor for a checkup, he told me, "You're morbidly obese. Do you know what 'morbidly obese' means?"

I mumbled, "That's what Homer is."

I'd hit 239 pounds, exactly Homer's weight. In the episode "Brush with Greatness" he crows, "I'm two-thirty-nine and I'm feeling fine!" I wrote that line.

(Sam wrote the next line. Mr. Burns says, "You're the fattest thing I've ever seen. And I've been on safari!")

I've since lost all that weight. You can read about it in my next book, *The "Don't Run* The Simpsons*" Diet.*

Cape Feare: The Musical?

Al and I ended our two years as showrunners with the episode "Cape Feare," in which Sideshow Bob gets out of prison to terrorize Bart. The show was based on a Robert De Niro movie, which was a remake of a Robert Mitchum movie, which was adapted from a John D. MacDonald novel. Just when you thought it couldn't get more derivative, someone turned our episode into an off-Broadway musical, *Mr. Burns: A Post-Electric Play,* a story of some postapocalyptic survivors who share only one cultural link: the "Cape Feare" episode of *The Simpsons.* They recreate the script and perform it as a traveling theater troupe. In act 2 we see their play seventy-five years later: it's become as ritualized and bizarre as a Greek Orthodox Mass. I'm always thrilled to see *The Simpsons* permeate pop culture, whether we're being parodied on *South Park* or rendered in oil paint by Ron

English. Plus, I loved the concept for this play. I couldn't wait to see it.

And then I saw it. Somehow they'd made *The Simpsons* three things it had never been before: grim, pretentious, and dull. It was so grim, pretentious, and dull that the New York theater critics loved it. I met the playwright after the show—she also struck me as G, P, & D. I said, "You're not a *Simpsons* fan, are you?"

"No, not really," she replied.

The only scenes people seemed to enjoy were the large hunks of our script that she used in the play—without crediting any of us. The whole thing made me furious on a daily basis; the theater was fifty yards from my front door and I had to pass it every day.

The play later opened in London, where the critics were less kind—one called it "three hours of utter Hell." God bless the Brits and their good taste. They gave us Chaplin. And Benny Hill.

WHAT IS A PRODUCER?

After thirty years on the air, *The Simpsons* has a bureaucracy as bloated and corrupt as the Italian parliament. The proof is that the show now has forty-seven producers.

Every writer on the show is called a producer. So is the guy who cuts the checks. And the casting agent. The showrunner, who works eighty hours a week, is a producer; but so is one guy who hasn't set foot in the office in fifteen years. And another guy who's been dead for three years. In short, some of our producers compose; others decompose.

CONAN O'BRIEN ON MIKE AND AL

"Al and Mike are very different personalities. They're both extremely hard workers, and they're both tenacious about getting the joke just right. And they both really want it to be good. They work their asses off, those guys. They don't settle, which is good. Also, they are not guys who are at the strip club at eleven o'clock at night. They have this work ethic. They're both fairly conservative—not politically, but in the way they live their lives. So in that sense, they're very similar. Al is a little more introverted and Mike is more of the transplanted vaudevillian comic. He's got an old-school delivery. If you could put him in a time machine and put him in Atlantic City in 1931, he could make a living and do pretty well as a comedian."

Padding

Occasionally on *The Simpsons*, you'll see a scene that's weird, even by our standards: it's not conventionally funny, and may have nothing to do with the story. Odds are, this scene is padding. One skill I learned at Harvard was how to stretch a five-page paper into a fifty-page thesis, and this served me well when I was running the show with Al Jean. For some reason, our episodes were always short, and we had to find a way to make the network minimum length: twenty minutes, twenty seconds.

One week, after editing the show "Lisa's First Word," we had an episode that was funny, touching, fast-paced . . . but thirty seconds too short to air. So Al and I wrote an extra-long couch gag—it ended with the back wall of the Simpsons' living room opening up into an elaborate Vegas stage show. (The opening credits of *Family Guy* look a lot like this couch gag. Just saying . . .) Though invented in desperation, the extended couch joke has become a creative mainstay of the show—we've done long couch gags many times since, and they are often fan favorites.

While people love an extra bit at the beginning, they're often baffled when it comes at the end. We once filled out a short show with a thirty-second cartoon called "The Adventures of Ned Flanders." It was hardly an adventure:

NED: Knock that off you two, it's time for church.

TODD FLANDERS: We're not going to church today!

NED: What? You give me one good reason.

TODD: It's Saturday!

NED: Okely dokely-doo!

Seconds after that aired, my father called. "What the hell was that?" he demanded. I didn't even know he watched *The Simpsons*.

Then there's the famous Sideshow Bob joke in "Cape Feare" that involves him stepping on an endless series of rakes. That alone was creative padding. But the show was still seven seconds short, so Al Jean said, "Let's do it again." We repeated the sequence exactly, and somehow turned a slapstick joke into a surreal classic.

Itchy and Scratchy cartoons are another great way to fill out a show. They're quick and funny, and they have no effect on the plot whatsoever. Bless their violent little hearts.

One padding trick we rarely use anymore is Bart's prank phone calls to Moe. They were freestanding scenes you could drop in anywhere, and they were a trademark of the show. However, these sequences were surprisingly hard to write—each one involved four separate jokes, which all had to be clever in their dumbness.

For example:

THE NAME: Amanda Hugginkiss

MOE MAKES IT WORSE: "Hey, I'm lookin' for Amanda Hugginkiss! Oh, why can't I find Amanda Hugginkiss?!"

THE PATRONS MAKE A REJOINDER: "Maybe your standards are too high!"

MOE THREATENS VENGEANCE: "You little SOB! Why, when I find out who you are, I'm going to shove a sausage down your throat and stick starving dogs up your butt!"

But the main reason we stopped doing these is that they never got a laugh at our table reads. Never.

One legendary attempt at show padding has been lost to the ages. Back in 1990, a second-season episode came in much too short, so we banged out a filler piece: "Nazis on Tap." It was supposedly a *Simpsons* cartoon short from the 1940s. It seemed like *The Simpsons,* but everything was just a little different: Mr. Burns owns an aircraft plant making planes for the war effort; Bart's spiky hair is replaced by a pointy Jughead cap; Moe the bartender is a dog, who asks, "Rrruff day at work, Homer?"

Matt Groening nixed the piece because it was too weird and too early in the series to just throw at people. I'm sure he wouldn't have a problem with it now.

Whether it's sitcoms or prom dresses, when padding's done right, it's a beautiful thing.

Interestingly, showrunner David Mirkin, who followed Al and me, had the opposite problem: his shows were often too long. Mirkin was always looking for tricks to jam a thirty-five-minute show into a thirty-minute slot. Someday you can read about it in his book, *Smirkin' with Mirkin.*

No Tech

If we have a guiding principle at *The Simpsons,* it's "If it ain't broke, don't fix it." Our cast members together earn $2 million per show—about half our production budget—but we'd never dream of replacing them with cheaper soundalikes. Most musical scores on TV shows simulate a symphonic sound with synthesizers, but we still use a full orchestra every week. It's slower, more expensive, and sounds just the same. So why do we do it? Because that's the way we've always done it.

The show is still drawn by hand—twenty-four thousand drawings per episode, to be exact. For fourteen years, it was also painted by hand, a slow, messy, expensive process. There were calls to switch over to computer ink-and-paint, but many feared the show might lose some character and warmth. So we did an experiment—one episode was picked at random ("Tennis the Menace," where the Simpsons get a tennis court), and the coloring was done by computer. We put it on the air to see if viewers could tell the difference, and if one person in America complained, we'd never use the process again. Nobody noticed, so we switched over to computer ink-and-paint—two years later.

You see, our other motto is "If it *is* broke, don't fix it, either." We have a single phone in the writers' office, and the 1 key doesn't work. It broke ten years ago and has never been repaired. So, to my mom in the 619 area code, sorry I haven't called.

CHAPTER SIX

MEET THE CHARACTERS

I used to be amazed by Matt Groening's gift for coining names for characters. In the early days of *The Simpsons,* they seemed to pour out of him:

The neighbor? *Flanders*

The reverend? *Lovejoy*

The mayor? *Quimby*

The bully? *Kearney*

Years later, I learned these were all street names in Matt's native Portland, Oregon. *Simpsons* characters have intentionally bland names, observing James Thurber's rule "[Humor] never recovers from such names as Ann S. Thetic, Maud Lynn, Sally Forth, Bertha Twins, and the like."

But there are interesting origins to some of the characters' names. Here are a few:

DR. JULIUS HIBBERT was originally a female doctor named Julia, whom writer Jay Kogen named after his friend Julia Hibbert. She later became famous under her maiden name, Julia Sweeney, as the creator of *SNL*'s "It's Pat" character.

PRINCIPAL SKINNER: Writer Jon Vitti named him after psychologist B. F. Skinner, inspired by rumors that B.F. used his children as lab rats for his theories. Vitti also named the school psychologist **DR. PRYOR** for his prying into the children's lives.

Bart's teacher is named **MRS. KRABAPPEL** (pronounced kruh-*BOP*-el), yet no student ever thinks to mock her as "Mrs. Crabapple." The joke here is that we *don't* do the joke. It's the same way Arnie Pye's helicopter traffic report is called "Arnie in the Sky" instead of the pun "Pye in the Sky." I'm not sure anyone ever gets these jokes. That includes me: ten years after Jeff Martin named Homer's barbershop quartet the Be Sharps, I looked at a piano and realized there is no B-sharp!

For no real reason, **JIMBO** the bully is named after our boss James L. Brooks. I'm not sure Jim is aware of this.

TROY McCLURE, Springfield's favorite has-been actor, was named after film star Troy Donahue and TV actor Doug Mc-Clure. Doug McClure's daughter Tané later told me that her father was a *Simpsons* fan. Upon seeing Troy's first appearance on the show, he asked his children, "Are they making fun of me?" Tané replied, "Yeah, Dad, I think they are." He watched a little longer, then remarked, "Well, it's pretty funny!" Subsequently, Doug's kids would call him Troy McClure behind his back.

MR. LARGO is the school music teacher named for a musical term. This is one of the rare funny names that stayed in the show (and it's not all that funny). Early on, Al Jean and I tried naming Mr. Burns "Mr. Meany." Another survivor is **HANS MOLEMAN,** who got his name after a writer exclaimed that the character "looks like a mole man!"

And one product, which is a character in itself:

DUFF BEER: We needed a name for Homer's favorite beer, and Jay Kogen came up with Duff. No, it was *not* named after Duff McKagan, bassist for Guns N' Roses; we'd never heard of this guy. Have you? McKagan loves to claim we called him and asked to use his name: "I knew nothing about branding yourself then or the royalties off it. I just thought cool, they wanna use my name and boom, *The Simpsons* was born. Yeah, if I had a nickel for every time . . . but it's fine." It's a cute fake story that McKagan tells in his aptly named memoir *It's So Easy: And Other Lies.*

Other Beloved Characters

BUMBLEBEE MAN: If you watch cable TV in Los Angeles, you have to click through thirty channels of Mexican television, and almost every one of these stations is showing a sitcom called *El Chapulín Colorado* (the Crimson Grasshopper) starring a guy in a ratty bug costume. Though we mock the character with Bumblebee Man, the Crimson Grasshopper gets ninety-one million viewers per episode in Mexico. We'd kill for that kind of number.

PROFESSOR FRINK: Frink is a pretty obvious rip-off—I mean homage—to Jerry Lewis in *The Nutty Professor.* Jay Kogen (again!) named the character after his friend John Frink. Years later, John Frink was hired as a writer on the show. After seeing the name in the credits, one viewer asked, "Are your characters coming to life now?" In 2003, when we needed an actor to play Frink's father, we got Jerry Lewis himself.

CHIEF WIGGUM: Some of our characters evolved from animals. Moe the bartender was modeled on a gorilla—note the hump in his back and his large muzzle. And Chief Wiggum was based on a pig; his voice is an homage to Edward G. Robinson. The fact that the police chief looks like a pig and talks like a gangster is our idea of deft social satire. Wiggum also manages to be dumber and fatter than Homer Simpson. That's why it scares me when police tell me, as they have many times, "You must have cops on staff. Because Chief Wiggum is so true to life."

KANG and KODOS, our resident aliens, have appeared in every Treehouse of Horror. They were inspired by aliens on the cover of a 1950s EC sci-fi comic in Sam Simon's office. Kang and Kodos originally closed *The Simpsons Movie,* appearing under the credits, debating the quality of the film:

KANG: At least the pig was cute.

KODOS: Yeah, until he vanished halfway through the picture!

Test audiences hated hearing aliens tear apart a film they'd just enjoyed—and the scene was cut.

ITCHY and SCRATCHY first appeared back in the *Tracey Ullman Show* shorts. They are not a parody of Tom and Jerry, but were actually inspired by Herman and Katnip, a cheap, ultraviolent knockoff of T&J (check them out on YouTube—they suck!). Sam Simon proudly came into our office one day to read the lyrics he'd written to the "Itchy & Scratchy" theme song:

> *They fight and bite*
> *They fight and bite and fight*
> *Fight fight fight*
> *Bite bite bite*
> *The Itchy & Scratchy Show!*

I can't say I was impressed, but over time Sam probably earned a million dollars in songwriting royalties from that. And despite Sam's huge contribution to Itchy and Scratchy lore, he always had to ask us, "Which one's the cat?" (Mnemonic device: Scratchy's the cat—his name contains the letters "C-A-T.")

People for years have asked when we're going to do an Itchy and Scratchy spin-off. To test out the possibility, our production team cut together every single "Itchy & Scratchy" short. It lasted just fourteen minutes—some of those cartoons are only nine seconds long—and contained such concentrated gore and mindless violence that it made people physically ill. Someone compared the assembled footage to the brainwashing films Alex had to watch in *A Clockwork Orange*.

(BONUS FACT: When we depict the writers of "Itchy & Scratchy" on the show, those are drawings of the current *Simpsons* writers. The disgusting, decrepit office they work in? That's our writers' room!)

BURNS'S LAWYER, the nasty blue-haired guy in glasses, was inspired by Roy Cohn, the horrible man who sent the Rosenbergs to the electric chair and defended Donald Trump. (Why couldn't it be the other way around?) The Roy Cohn voice is done by Dan Castellaneta, one of his many spot-on impressions of obscure celebrities. (Sam Simon said they hired Dan at *The Tracey Ullman Show* after he did an impression of playwright Edward Albee. No one knew what Albee actually sounded like, but they took Dan's word for it.)

Mr. Burns's loyal assistant **SMITHERS** used to be African American. The first season of the show, Smithers was black—well, actually greenish-brown, in *The Simpsons'* weird color palette. It was only when we saw those early shows in color that it seemed wrong to have a prominent black character kissing up to his cruel white boss. So we went *Poof! He's white.*

(TIDBIT: Skin color has always been a problem on the show. Once we instructed our Korean animators not to make all background characters white. In the next show they animated, all the homeless people and criminals were black.)

Midway through the second season, Sam walked into our offices and announced "Smithers is gay. Don't mention it directly, don't make jokes about it, just have it in your minds when you're writing the character." Even this was a bold move—back in 1991, there were no gay characters on network television.

Soon after those shows started airing, a BBC reporter flew in from London, plopped himself on my couch, and said, "I'm here to talk about Smithers." Years later, when we needed a first name for Smithers, I dubbed him **WAYLON,** in honor of iconic gay ventriloquist Wayland Flowers (and Madame).

So Smithers is the first man in history to go from black and straight to white and gay.

The second was Michael Jackson.

Character Origins

Our characters are created the same way babies are created—by accident. Almost all our characters first appear in the script, vaguely described, with a joke or two. Then our actors find a funny voice to go with the line, and our animators draw a character that fits the voice. If all that makes us laugh when we see it animated, a character is born.

A case in point is Groundskeeper Willie—in his first appearance back in 1991 he had two lines in the script: "You'll be back," and later, "I told you you'd be back." These were the last two lines we were recording at the end of a long day. Dan Castellaneta asked us who the character was. Sam Simon replied, "I don't know. Give him an accent." We tried the character Hispanic, but that seemed clichéd, so Dan made him Scottish. Forty-five seconds: that's how much thought went into making Groundskeeper Willie Scottish.

He's now a national hero in Scotland.

In fact, in one episode we said Willie is from Glasgow and in another we said he's from Aberdeen. Why? Because we didn't give a crap.

But people in Aberdeen and Glasgow care deeply. When these two cities play each other in soccer, a riot breaks out—legs are broken, ears are bitten. Poet Lord Byron was from Aberdeen. Scientist Lord Kelvin was from Glasgow. But these towns are fighting over bragging rights for a drunken cartoon janitor who lives in a shack.

Some characters change over time. Al Jean and I created Ralph, but we meant him to be a mini Homer—we named him after Jackie Gleason's character Ralph Kramden. As years passed, Ralph evolved into this sort of brain-dead Buddha. And it wasn't until season 4 that we decided to make him Chief Wiggum's son. It's a cartoon—we can do that.

Hank Azaria may be the best at creating a character from nothing: he once gave a very funny reading to the line "Just stamp the ticket," which became our recurring character Just Stamp the Ticket Man.

My Favorite Character to Write

Homer is God's gift to comedy writers. He's fat. He's bald. He's a stupid, lazy drunk with anger issues. He's exhibited all seven deadly sins: pride, greed, lust, envy, gluttony, wrath, and sloth.

In "Lisa's Pony," Homer walks into a pet shop (All Creatures Great and Cheap) and the owner remarks, "Oh my, what is that smell?" Writer George Meyer remarked, "Oh. I guess Homer smells now, too."

But despite his many, many, many, many, many, many flaws, Homer is a good guy. He has moments of true tenderness. He loves his wife and two of his three kids.

We acknowledge Homer's forebears with his "muzzle": this is

what we call the permanent five o'clock shadow that he sports. It's a tribute to Fred Flintstone, who had the same beard line. It's no accident that Fred and Homer both have best friends named Barney. I gave Barney the last name Gumble, to honor two cartoon sidekicks: Barney Rubble and Snuffy Smith's pal Barney Google.

My runner-up for favorite character is Grampa. Here's why: Every kid in the world watches *The Simpsons*. High school kids, college students watch *The Simpsons*. Parents now watch the show with their kids.

Not one old person on earth watches our show. So when we make fun of Grampa, we're not offending one viewer. In fact, this is the reason our ratings go up every year—because the people who don't watch our show are dying.

And I think that's great.

Is Apu Taboo?

I always liked Apu. We all work very hard at *The Simpsons,* and Apu is the only person in Springfield who works hard at his job. Plus, he's always in a good mood, and when you pitch lines for him, it puts you in a good mood. His voice always has an upbeat musical cadence (sing it):

> *Hello, Mr. Homer*
> *How you doing, Mr. Homer?*
> *Have a Squishee.*
> *Have a hot dog.*
> *Have a good day.*
> *Come again.*

Apu first appeared in the 1990 episode "The Telltale Head." In the script, he had the generic name Clerk, and a single forgettable line, "Thirty-five cents, please." Because Hindu convenience store clerks were a movie comedy cliché even back then, I inserted this stage direction under his line: (THE CLERK IS NOT INDIAN). When we got to the cast reading of the script, Hank Azaria read the Clerk with an Indian accent and got a huge laugh. That's how the Clerk became Indian, and that's when I concluded that Hank doesn't read stage directions.

Or so I thought for years . . . Hank recently revealed that it was Sam Simon's idea to read the part with the accent.

Once the character became an Indian, we had to give him a name. Matt Groening chose Apu, honoring the Apu Trilogy of films, directed by Satyajit Ray. His last name, Nahasapeemapetilon is actually the full name of a high school classmate of *Simpsons* writer Jeff Martin.

We always tried to write Apu with depth and dignity, but I still worried what Indians thought of him. Finally, four years after the character was created, I asked my friend Priya, "What do you think of Apu?"

She said, "He's the only Indian on television."

That was 1994. She was happy to be represented on TV.

Since then, there are a lot more Indians on TV: in *The Big Bang Theory, Master of None,* any medical show you can think of (the Indian doctor is becoming its own stereotype, albeit a positive one).

But recently, we've heard more and more complaints about Apu, mostly from the generation of young Indians who grew up watching the character. Many say they were taunted in the schoolyard by being called Apu.

That's not racism. That's just saying *kids are dicks.* Still, we hate bullies on *The Simpsons* (even though we have four of them as characters).

Sure, Hank Azaria is not Indian. But almost no one on our show plays what they are: white guys play black men, straights play gays, and grown women play little boys. And Apu might be an unflattering stereotype, but that can be said about lots of our characters, from Grampa to Rich Texan. Groundskeeper Willie is pure cliché: a whiskey-swilling, haggis-eating, bagpipe-playing Scotsman—played by an Italian actor. And yet, as I mentioned before, the Scottish people love him. Maybe it's because he's the only Scotsman on television.

There have been enough complaints about Apu to fill an angry little documentary, *The Problem with Apu*, released in November 2017. (The doc ends with filmmaker Hari Kondabolu beating up a cardboard cutout of Hank Azaria. *An Inconvenient Truth*, in contrast, did not end with Al Gore strangling a piece of carbon.) We don't really disagree with Hari's point—in fact, we made it ourselves, twenty-three months earlier. We did an episode in January 2016 called "Much Apu About Something," in which Apu's nephew (played by Utkarsh Ambudkar) calls him a stereotype. After that, we quietly benched Apu. The press didn't notice; not even Hari Kondabolu noticed. It was only when I mentioned this fact in an interview that Apu-lovers got upset. It's something that unites Apu-lovers and Apu-haters: None of them realizes that Apu has barely said a word in three years.

For now, Apu is neither in the show nor out of it: He's Schrodinger's character. I have no idea what, if anything, *The Simpsons* producers will do. It's not my call: As a white Jewish guy, I can't tell Indians not to be offended by another white Jewish guy playing an Indian.

Making the Big D'oh

The Simpsons has many famous catchphrases, but only one is truly original. We took Bart's "cowabunga" from Chief Thunderthud on *The Howdy Doody Show*. "Eat my shorts" is a line Nancy Cartwright improvised, remembering it from her high school band days. The "Caramba" in "*ay caramba*" was a Portuguese flamenco dancer. "Don't have a cow" dates back to the fifties—it's a variant on the British phrase "don't have kittens."

Our most popular catchphrase is Homer's "d'oh," but even that's not original. It came from thirties film comedian Jimmy Finlayson, and he said it as a euphemism for "damn." "D'oh" is so popular, it made it into the *Oxford English Dictionary*, though misspelled as "doh" (you can't even trust the OED).

We actually write it in scripts as (ANNOYED GRUNT). Dan Castellaneta saw that stage direction and read it as "D'oh!" Sometimes we write intentionally challenging stage directions, like (CONFUSED ANNOYED GRUNT THAT SUDDENLY TURNS AMOROUS). Whatever we throw at him, Dan can do it.

What's the one original catchphrase on *The Simpsons*? Nelson Muntz's "haw-haw." It first appeared in a John Swartzwelder script, "The War of the Simpsons": Grampa, threatening to whip Nelson, takes off his belt . . . and Grampa's pants fall down! Nelson says, for the first time, "Haw-haw!" There are a million ways to read that word, but the way Nancy Cartwright did it was as a two-note bray: E-sharp, C-sharp. That first "haw-haw" produced an explosion of laughter at the table read, and a classic was born.

TRUE FACT!

There is a guy living in Macon, Georgia, whose name is Homer Simpson . . . and he works in a nuclear power plant! That poor guy. Having to live in Macon, Georgia.

CHAPTER SEVEN

MEET THE CAST

One day, while recording the show, Dan Castellaneta (Homer) and Nancy Cartwright (Bart) were horsing around, when Julie Kavner (Marge) told them to cut it out. Meanwhile, Yeardley Smith (Lisa) moaned that we'd never get the work done in time. Sam Simon leaned over to me and whispered, "They're just like their characters."

There is definitely some truth to that, but they're a pretty diverse group, and they all got their jobs in different ways. Dan Castellaneta and Julie Kavner were cast members on *The Tracey Ullman Show;* when the Simpsons shorts became part of that series in the second season, Dan was given the role of Homer. Tracey Ullman herself was going to play Marge, but the show kept her too busy; Julie got the role instead. Nancy Cartwright, already an accomplished voice actress in 1986, auditioned for the role of Lisa and wound up as Bart. Yeardley Smith, who'd never done voice-over, came in for Bart and wound up as Lisa.

We now had the Simpson family, but when the cartoon shorts expanded to a half-hour series, we needed additional actors to fill out the rest of Springfield. Matt Groening suggested Harry Shearer; Matt was a fan of his NPR series *Le Show,* in which Harry played multiple roles week after week. Harry's our most experienced actor: he started out as a child star, working with Jack Benny and Abbott and Costello. (Check out *Abbott and Costello Go to Mars*—a young Harry appears in the first ten minutes. He's instantly recognizable and hilarious.)

Hank Azaria was the last of our main cast members to join *The Simpsons.* We had already recorded our first episode when we brought him in as a replacement Moe. (Christopher Collins originated the character, but the producers wanted a different voice.) Hank's previous voice acting experience consisted of exactly one job: the title role of *Hollywood Dog* in a failed Fox pilot. Hank was brought back, episode by episode, during *The Simpsons'* first season; he joined the cast full time in our second year. Since he's been a regular for only twenty-nine of our thirty seasons, Matt Groening calls Hank "the new guy."

Let's learn more about the cast . . .

Dan Castellaneta
(Homer, Barney, Grampa, Krusty)

Except for male pattern baldness, Dan has absolutely nothing in common with Homer. Dan is modest, soft-spoken, even-tempered, and deeply intelligent. He plays dozens of characters on the show, but stumbles only when reading Homer's lines—it's like he's channeling his inner dyslexic. Of the three men in our cast, he's the only Gentile, so obviously we made him voice Krusty, our main Jewish character.

Julie Kavner
(Marge, Patty, Selma)

Julie naturally found Marge's raspy voice after a grueling week of rehearsals on *The Tracey Ullman Show*. When she's asked why Marge loves Homer despite all his faults (and she's asked that a lot!), she replies, "He's good in bed." I don't think she's kidding.

Early in the show, Julie asked Jim Brooks how she should differentiate the voices of Patty and Selma. Jim replied, "Don't."

Nancy Cartwright
(Bart, Nelson, Ralph)

Not since Lassie had a TV actor played a classic character of the opposite sex. Nancy Cartwright has three of them: in Nelson, Bart, and Ralph she embodies the id, the ego, and the superego of American boyhood. (There's some high-class academic bullshit for you!) Nancy is so bouncy and vivacious that it seems natural when Bart's voice comes out of her—except for a couple of times when she was eight months pregnant. She'd say, "Don't have a cow, man," and she looked like she was literally going to have a cow. (Now she's a grandmother!)

Yeardley Smith (Lisa)

Dan may do thirty characters on the show and Harry may do fifty, but Yeardley does one. But what a character! For many of us, Lisa is the heart and soul of the show, the source of its emotional depth. Yeardley shares enough of Lisa's anxieties and insecurities to fill a one-woman show—her funny, touching, and occasionally harrowing stage presentation called *More*.

Hank Azaria
(Moe, Apu, Chief Wiggum, Comic Book Guy)

Hank has an amazing gift for creating memorable characters from small parts, which is why many of them don't exactly have names: Comic Book Guy, Bumblebee Man, Old Jewish Man, Sea Captain, Wise Guy. He claims some of them are just really bad impersonations of famous acting icons, including Moe (Al Pacino), Dr. Nick Riviera (Desi Arnaz), and Lou the cop (Sylvester Stallone). Hank has a special link to Chief Wiggum: When Hank has to learn a song for a role, he sings it in Wiggum's voice first. Says Hank, "I have more faith in Wiggum's voice than my own." You haven't heard "Let It Go" from *Frozen* till you've heard Hank sing it as Chief Wiggum. A million people have already viewed it on YouTube.

Harry Shearer
(Mr. Burns, Smithers, Ned Flanders,
Dr. Hibbert, Kent Brockman)

Harry is enormously proud that he plays both the nicest guy in Springfield (Ned) and the meanest (Mr. Burns), as well as providing the voices of both God and Satan. That's range! Those long dialogue scenes between Burns and Smithers are just Harry talking to himself, effortlessly switching between characters, and in thirty years, I've never seen him make a mistake once. In 2016, it looked like Harry might not come back to the show. Senator Ted Cruz, in the midst of his presidential run, auditioned for his roles. You can see that on YouTube, too: "Ted Cruz Auditions for *The Simpsons*." Needless to say, that's two jobs Cruz didn't get that year.

(Left to right:) Dan Castellaneta, Harvey Weinstein, and me.

Special Mention: Phil Hartman

Phil Hartman would roll into *Simpsons* recordings with the easy-going charm of a door-to-door salesman. He could be both sincere and a parody of sincerity at the same time. As Conan O'Brien pointed out, "There's no difference between Phil Hartman and a Phil Hartman robot."

Phil brought this android-like quality to his performances—he'd make the long drive from Malibu to Fox and record his lines perfectly on the first take. I couldn't bear the thought that he'd driven ninety minutes to do five minutes' work; I'd always have him do extra takes just to make it worth his while. I wouldn't see that level of perfection again until two decades later, when Stephen Colbert guested on the show. He played a very Phil Hartman-esque life coach, and he nailed every line immediately.

Phil contributed two indelible characters to *The Simpsons:* sleazy lawyer Lionel Hutz and washed-up actor Troy McClure.

They had exactly the same voice. This was never a problem until the time we wrote a scene featuring both Lionel and Troy. Phil tried gamely to differentiate the two characters, but I told him not to bother.

Phil was murdered the week *Futurama* recorded its pilot, in which he was supposed to voice arrogantly stupid space hero Zapp Brannigan. Instead, the character is played by Billy West, doing his best version of Phil Hartman.

But there's no replacing Phil. We didn't even try. After he died, we retired Lionel Hutz and Troy McClure forever.

Bonus Voice Actor Factoid:
Pamela Hayden

She's cute, sexy, flirtatious, and . . . Milhouse. It's a little disturbing.

The Case of the Vanishing Julie

The cast of *The Simpsons* appeared on *Inside the Actors Studio* in 2003. It was a great show and a remarkable coup getting them all in one place: While half of them live in Los Angeles, Hank Azaria is in New York, Harry Shearer's in New Orleans, and Julie Kavner spends much of the year in Michigan. On top of that, both Julie and Dan Castellaneta don't like to be filmed doing their characters—they feel it robs Homer and Marge of their realism. (Paul Fusco felt the same way—during the entire run of *ALF*, he never let it be known he was the voice and puppeteer of the alien.)

The Bravo network was so proud of this *Actors Studio* episode that they seemed to air it day and night for the next decade. It was on so often that even casual viewers noticed a weird detail: Julie Kavner vanishes in the middle of the show! She's there, and suddenly she's gone, and none of the other actors comment on it. Many, many fans have asked me what happened.

The night of the taping, Julie told the Bravo producers that she had to catch a plane in three hours. They told her that shouldn't be a problem: the show runs just over an hour. What they didn't say is that they tape for four hours, and then cut it down to the best sixty-five minutes. One cast member told me that when James Lipton brought out his prepared questions, they were on a stack of index cards six inches thick.

Julie stayed for as long as she could, but when her time ran out, so did she. It's a disappearing act worthy of Houdini.

NANCY CARTWRIGHT ON VOICE DIRECTION

"I'd been working professionally for years before *The Simpsons*, doing *My Little Pony, Pound Puppies, Snorks, Ri¢hie Ri¢h* . . . That was Saturday-morning syndicated television. There was just a certain way of doing it. So I was just kind of shocked that the *Simpsons writers* were directing us! And it was taking *all day*. We were there from ten in the morning until about nine o'clock at night. That was just not done. It was an extraordinary amount of time. And yet I am so glad I kept my big mouth shut. Because what ended up evolving from that particular procedure was *genius*. At the same time, any suggestion that I would have or any ad-libs that I did, the writers appreciated. Because we were a team! We were absolutely a collaborative team."

. . . Now, Meet the Guest Stars

If you believe Wikipedia, *The Simpsons* had 725 guest stars in its first twenty-six seasons. Of course, according to Wikipedia, I've had sex with 725 supermodels. I know because I put it there.

Guest stars have been a part of the show since the pilot, when **Penny Marshall** played the Babysitter Bandit. In that same episode, **William Shatner** became the first celebrity to turn down a guest shot on *The Simpsons,* when we offered him a role parodying himself (if that's possible).

Our guest stars have come from the world of acting (**Glenn Close**), music (three of the **Beatles**—John won't return our calls), science (**Stephen Hawking**), literature (**J. K. Rowling**), comedy (**Joan Rivers**), and tragedy (**Jon Lovitz**). There were even serious actors who were really funny (*MacGyver*'s **Richard Dean Anderson**). Best of all, there were guests who acted exactly like themselves in person (**Larry King,** who spent twenty minutes talking to me about bagels).

All this **bold-faced name-dropping** gets old fast. **Jesus.**

Thomas Pynchon, an author who hasn't been photographed or interviewed in half a century, appeared on *The Simpsons.* Twice. The first time, he plays against his image, yelling at passersby, "Hey, over here! Have your picture taken with a reclusive author!" The second time he appeared, he even wrote jokes for himself. After landing Pynchon and getting the equally mysterious artist Banksy to animate our couch gag, we offered a part to the granddaddy of all recluses: J. D. Salinger. We approached him through his son, actor Matt Salinger. (He played a jock in *Revenge of the Nerds.*) J. D. Salinger gave us the quickest rejection we ever got: forty-five seconds.

Johnny Carson went from being omnipresent to reclusive. After he left *The Tonight Show,* he made only two TV appearances: on the American Teachers Awards presentation . . . and us. We'd heard from a friend who was working for him that Carson said, "Gee, they got all these big celebrities on *The Simpsons*—why don't they ask me?" So we did.

We wrote a storyline where a postretirement Carson comes to visit the Simpsons . . . and won't leave. He becomes the bad brother-in-law: sleeping on their couch, stealing the last piece of pizza, drinking Homer's beer.

Carson was deeply offended and turned down the part. The writing staff was ready to give up on him, but I urged them to try another approach—instead of making Johnny a slob, let's make him a superhero. We wrote a scene where he appeared on *The Krusty the Clown Show,* singing opera and juggling a Chrysler with one hand. Carson accepted. He rolled into our studio early one morning, did a little monologue for us about the previous night's Emmys (Johnny had won one, but didn't show up), recorded his lines, charmed everyone, and signed autographs for the next two hours.

There was a funny piece of dialogue from the episode that got cut. After Johnny juggles the car, Krusty asks:

KRUSTY: Wow, Johnny! How come you never did this on your show?

CARSON: Suzanne Pleshette ran long.

Other *Tonight Show* hosts—Leno, Conan, all the way back to Steve Allen—also did our show. Steve, though clearly a brilliant man, needed nine takes to do the line "*Ay caramba.*" We finally used the "*ay*" from take six and the "*caramba*" from take three.

Dustin Hoffman appeared in the episode "Lisa's Substitute," playing, well, Lisa's substitute. His character, Mr. Bergstrom, was based on a teacher I had by the same name. My Mr. Bergstrom had a deformed hand, so I asked the animators to give the character some sort of humanizing deformity. The deformity they gave him? They made him look exactly like me. Sam Simon designed the character, modeling Bergstrom's Semitic good looks (meaning bad looks) on mine. Hoffman asked that we not use his name in the credits, so we called him Sam Etic, a terrible pun on Semitic. To recap: Mr. Bergstrom has Dustin's voice and my face, but Sam Etic gets all the credit.

Here's a trivia question: if Mr. Bergstrom was played by a two-time Oscar winner, what character was *voiced* by a four-time Oscar winner?

Maggie Simpson. She rarely speaks, but whenever she does, she's voiced by a guest star: Elizabeth Taylor, Jodie Foster, and Carol Kane. The actresses playing Maggie have won four Oscars and been nominated ten times.

Liz Taylor played Maggie back in 1992, uttering the baby's first word. Liz created the biggest stir of any guest we've had on the show. Three hundred people packed our tiny studio to hear her record her one-word part: "Daddy." She had to do six takes because, as you can imagine, it kept coming out too sexy. We had to remind her she was a baby talking to her father, not hitting on him. Liz did hit on one guy in the crowded room—our animation supervisor, David Silverman. "Who is that?" she purred. Silverman was the handsomest guy in the room, but then, compared to *Simpsons* writers, Paul Giamatti would have also won that prize.

All of this raises the pertinent question: Why do we even use guest stars? After all, our cast can imitate anyone on earth. In fact, we once wrote a whole show for Woody Allen, but Dan Castellaneta did such a spot-on impression at rehearsals, we decided, "Who needs Woody?"

Truth is, we often write in guest stars to meet our idols. The writers have used the show to bring in all of their comedy heroes: Eric Idle, Rodney Dangerfield, Albert Brooks, Mel Brooks, Jerry and Richard Lewis. Ricky Gervais, who sort of invented modern comedy with the original version of *The Office,* asked us if he could write an episode. We were flattered, and even more flattered when he called back two weeks later and said, "I can't do it—it's too hard." (He did pitch the plot of the show, star in it, and perform original songs.)

We were all fans of *Girls,* so Lena Dunham was a natural choice. But it hadn't occurred to us until I sat behind her on a plane and heard her talking; her voice was perfect for animation. We also cast German director Werner Herzog—not your typical cartoon guest star—after hearing his one-of-a-kind voice on a documentary.

We get a guest star when it's appropriate: if we do an opera show, we get Plácido Domingo; a tennis show, Pete Sampras. We had nine Major League Baseball players in our softball show, and every single famous magician alive on our magic episode. We even got Teller (the silent half of Penn &) to talk!

Sometimes it's not so appropriate. Like in the episode where Homer goes to space, our guest stars were Buzz Aldrin and . . . James Taylor? What can I say? We wanted to meet the guy.

Then there's the time we asked George Takei from *Star Trek* to play himself in our monorail episode—Takei had been on an earlier episode, playing a sushi chef, and he loved it. But Takei turned us down, saying (do your best Takei impression here): "I don't make fun of monorails." Turns out he's an impassioned fan of public transit. Instead, we went to Leonard Nimoy, who happily took the part. How often do you ask for Sulu and wind up with Spock?

It can get weirder than that. We once wrote a part for a random celebrity. We asked our casting agent for suggestions and she said, "[Celebrity I can't name] owes Fox four hundred bucks, and that's what we pay our guest stars. He can work off the debt." I don't know what this legendary performer did to run up this tab—steal a computer? Whatever it was, he made for a fun, surprising choice for the role.

Except for that guy, no celebrity does *The Simpsons* for the money. So why do they do it? First off, it's easy. Even a leading guest role doesn't take more than an hour to record, and there's no wardrobe or makeup to worry about. Plus, the celebrity can come in at his or her convenience, anytime during a two-month window. Or not come in at all—we've recorded guest stars in their homes, in their cars, and over the phone.

But there are other reasons:

- 🍺 **THEY LIKE THE SHOW.** The reason we had so few older guest stars on the early episodes is because senior citizens never watched our show. For one episode, we offered the role of God to Burt Lancaster, Charlton Heston, and Gregory Peck, who all said no. Years later, Kirk Douglas appeared on our show as a con man. He had a stroke shortly after, making this *Simpsons* role his last lusty, full-throated Kirk Douglas performance.

- 🍺 **THEIR KIDS MAKE THEM DO IT.** No explanation needed here.

- 🍺 **THEY'RE FRIENDS OF THE PRODUCERS.** Jim Brooks has brought in as guest stars half the cast of his old series *The Mary Tyler Moore Show*: Cloris Leachman, Ed Asner, Betty White, and Valerie Harper. Jay Kogen delivered his friends Phil Hartman and Jon Lovitz from the comedy troupe the Groundlings. Sam Simon drew on his days at *Cheers* to cast Kelsey Grammer as Sideshow Bob.

  Kelsey is every bit as smart as the characters he plays—we've never written a Sideshow Bob line so esoteric that he didn't get it. And although he's not as evil as Bob, Kelsey is a staunch Republican. And like Sideshow Bob, he did a little jail time in the eighties. I was directing him in a scene where Bob is being shoved into a prison cell and said, "I need you to make a noise like you're being roughed up by cops."

"Oh, I can do that," he said with a grin.

The Quarter-Century Audition: William Friedkin

Back in 1992 we were writing our "Mr. Plow" episode when we heard a rumor that Oscar-winning director William Friedkin (*The French Connection, The Exorcist*) was a huge fan of the show. "Let's write a joke just for him," we decided. This was the only time we ever did a gag for a single viewer: we threw in a shot of Homer's snowplow driving on a rickety rope bridge, right out of Friedkin's film *Sorcerer*. A quarter century later, I finally met the

William Friedkin finally gets to meet Nancy "Bart" Cartwright. Matt Groening photobombs.

guy and told him about our joke. Friedkin had seen it and he loved it! I invited him to our next *Simpsons* table read, and he showed up with a guest, the bishop of Los Angeles. Mr. Friedkin ("Call me Billy!") proceeded to charm everyone in the place and created a sensation like I hadn't seen since Liz Taylor's visit. We immediately wrote him a guest role in our 2017 Treehouse of Horror.

He finally got a spot on our show. And it only took twenty-five years.

My Favorite Guest Star

We had heavyweight champ Joe Frazier on the show in 1992. We sent George Meyer, the writing staff's biggest boxing fan, to record him. I wasn't even at the session, but I listened to the tape of it over and over.

Joe's line was "We now present the Montgomery Burns Award for Outstanding Achievement in the Field of Excellence." We should have realized that Frazier had never uttered a sentence that long in his life; he had whole press conferences that were shorter than this line. It was an ungainly sentence that Olivier might have had trouble with. Joe immediately was struggling with the line, so George Meyer decided to break it into smaller bits.

FRAZIER: We now present the . . .

GEORGE: Cut! Perfect! Keep going, champ.

FRAZIER: Montgomery . . .

GEORGE: Fantastic! You're a natural!

Frazier fought his way through the line, one phrase at a time. Punch for punch, jab for jab, he was nailing it. It all went beautifully until his final word: *Excellence.* Frazier asked, "Is that 'excellent'? Or 'excel-lunch'?" He didn't know the term *excellence,* but seemed to think *excellunch* was a word.

GEORGE: It's excel-lence. *Lence.* Like a contact *lens.*

FRAZIER: (LONG, BAFFLED PAUSE)

GEORGE: Look, we can change this to another word . . .

FRAZIER: No! I can do this!

Listening to his determination is truly what made Joe Frazier my favorite guest star. I saw what made him a champ. He never gave up, whether he was fighting with Muhammad Ali or wrestling with a three-syllable word. He was going to get this line right if it took him twenty takes.

And he did finally get it right. Twenty takes later.

GUEST STAR MEMORIES: DAVID COPPERFIELD

"Obviously, I did the magic episode. It was really, really fun. And the best thing in the world is to be asked back. When the audience comes back to see you a second time, that's a good thing. I got to do it a second time, reprising my role as me, and I just love doing this show with these really smart, smart people doing crazy stuff. It's very rewarding."

Michael Jackson: Super Guest Star

In 1991, Michael Jackson called Matt Groening and said he wanted to do *The Simpsons.* Michael was at the peak of his superduperstardom at the time—as big as the Beatles in the days of Beatlemania, and no performer I can recall has since been quite so huge. The whole staff was tasked with coming up with ideas for an episode, and Jim Brooks had the best: Homer is put in a mental institution, where his cellmate is a three-hundred-pound white guy who thinks he's Michael Jackson (with Michael doing the voice).

Al Jean and I were assigned the script, and we started with an outline—a twenty-page single-spaced story synopsis. It was a dry, nearly unreadable document, but Jackson read it, and offered some funny suggestions: he pitched the scene where Bart tells the town that Michael Jackson is coming to visit, creating an uproar; and he added the scene where "Michael" writes a song with Bart. (He also made us change a joke about Prince to be about Elvis!) Al and I were showrunners at the time, so we wrote this script after hours, generally starting work at eleven P.M. It was a real grind, and neither of us thought Michael would actually do the show.

We had the script reading at the home of Michael's manager Sandy Gallin. It was a mansion so large, Gallin remarked, "You know, I still haven't seen every room in my house." I sat next to Michael at the reading and was three feet away from him as he sang "Ben," "Thriller," and the song he composed for the episode, "Lisa, It's Your Birthday." I couldn't wait till we got that performance on tape.

Michael came into our studios a few days later to record the show. He was alone—no entourage—and was strikingly handsome. (This was about three nose jobs before the end.) I was also surprised by how tall and strong he appeared. (It was a sad realization that Michael Jackson could kick my ass.) He was very friendly and shook everyone's hand. As we were about to start the recording, Sam Simon announced, "I'd like to have a big *Simpsons* round of applause for Michael"—Jackson smiled humbly—"Reiss, who just won fifty dollars playing *Phone Jeop-*

ardy!" Jackson looked baffled at first, then nicely joined in the applause.

Jim Brooks stepped in to personally direct Michael. But Michael was no actor, and Jim is not the only Oscar-winning director to try to squeeze a good performance out of him: Martin Scorsese in the "Bad" video and Francis Ford Coppola in "Captain EO" both tried in vain to make Michael look badass.

If Michael's acting wasn't great, at least his singing would be. We'd recorded all of Michael's spoken parts in the morning, and we would finish the day with the songs. And that's when Michael called in a little white guy. "This is Kipp Lennon—he's my authorized soundalike." (For you old-timers, Kipp is the brother of the singing group the Lennon Sisters.) Michael stood by laughing as Kipp performed all the songs in that episode. It's an amazing impression, but if you watch the show again, you can tell that Kipp is actually spoofing Michael, to Jackson's delight.

We asked Jackson, "Um, Michael . . . why are you doing this?"

He replied cryptically, "It's a joke on my brothers."

Let me be the first to say it: Michael Jackson was an odd guy.

GUEST STAR MEMORIES: JON LOVITZ

"I thought the 'Streetcar' episode I was in was a really funny show. It was so funny that I still remember some of the lines. I played the director Llewellyn Sinclair: 'I have directed three plays in my career, and I have had three heart attacks. That's how much I care—I'm planning for a fourth.' I remember the first time I was doing the read-through, and they would be dying laughing the moment I opened my mouth. I remember thinking, *Gee, they REALLY think I'm funny!*"

Guest Stars We Can't Get

We've asked Bruce Springsteen to do the show repeatedly, but he always turns us down. We sent him a *Simpsons* jacket as a bribe, which didn't work. We even had his sax player, Clarence Clemons, on the show, hoping he'd tell Bruce how much fun it was. That didn't work, either.

Bruce, we'd like our jacket back.

It was odd, because rock stars rarely turn us down. We've had so many on the show that when we wanted to open *The Simpsons Movie* with a musical act, we said, "Who's left? We've had them all." I finally pushed for Green Day because I wanted free Green Day tickets. They did the movie and now get requests to do their version of the *Simpsons* theme at concerts. Or so I hear; I never got my free tickets.

We've had the mayor of New York (Rudolph Giuliani) and the prime minister of the UK (Tony Blair). We had Giuliani delivering the commencement address at a school for police dogs. He told us, "You know, I've actually had to do this." As for Blair, he recorded his role at the same time he was deciding to enter the Iraq War. This is proof that you shouldn't try to do two things at once.

What we've never had is a U.S. president. Gerald Ford was our first ask; we were going to show him working in the Gerald Ford Presidential Library, stamping books and shaking down patrons for fifteen-cent late fees, but he turned us down. Every president from Ford to Obama rejected us; Michelle Obama turned us down, too.

The closest we ever came was Bill Clinton. After we wrote him a part and sent him the script, he notified us, "While I'd love to do *The Simpsons,* I'd never do anything to disgrace the office of the president." Sometimes they write the jokes for you.

And then there's the story I heard from Jimmy Carter's grandson himself. As a kid, the grandson was always urging Grampa

Jimmy to watch *The Simpsons*: "You'll like it—it's smart and satirical." One week, Jimmy Carter decided to watch our show. It was the episode where Springfield has budget cuts, so instead of getting a statue of Abraham Lincoln for the park, they get the much cheaper Jimmy Carter statue. When it's unveiled, a riot breaks out, with someone calling Jimmy Carter "history's greatest monster."

Needless to say, Jimmy Carter will never do our show.

Tom Cruise was an early fan of our show—tapes of new episodes were sent to him when he was filming on location. And so we wrote a role just for him: he was supposed to play "Tom," the Top Gun pilot in "Brother from the Same Planet." Cruise turned down the part, so we gave the role to Phil Hartman in what became a classic episode. Tom turned us down, but he did *The Mummy*. Go figure.

In Alec Guinness's memoir *A Positively Final Appearance*, we learned he was a big *Simpsons* fan. Unfortunately, we read this in 2001, and Guinness passed away the year before. D'oh! Why didn't he tell us? The same thing happened with Stanley Kubrick: we didn't find out he was a fan until after he died.

There are three celebrities who've asked to be on *The Simpsons* but, after we wrote a part for them, turned it down: Prince, George Lucas, and Lyle Lovett. Okay, two celebrities and Lyle Lovett.

Prince was eager to do the show until he saw the script we'd written for him: he was to reprise the role of Leon Kompowsky. The three-hundred-pound mental patient who thought he was Michael Jackson was back—and now he thought he was Prince. The real Prince said no thanks, and the script was burned.

George Lucas told a friend he wanted to do our show, so we wrote him a very funny part. Lucas would be hanging around Comic Book Guy, always talking about *Star Wars* but not quite getting it right: "We're like those two on the spaceship: the big dog and the guy in the vest." Lucas turned down the part. But we had our revenge . . .

A few years later, we parodied the lousy *Star Wars* prequels (*Cosmic Wars* featuring Jim-Jam Bonks), and we depicted the films' creator as a three-foot-tall gnome who looked like George Lucas. The parody was so vicious that the day after it aired, the *Simpsons* writers showed an emotion I'd never seen from them before: remorse. Al Jean sighed. "We didn't have to make him *that* short."

GUEST STAR MEMORIES: JUDD APATOW

"Then they did an episode in which my wife, Leslie Mann; Paul Rudd; and I did voices. You don't get better career highs than *that*. I went into the studio to record it, and James Brooks pitched me incredible lines. I know that Seth Rogen and Evan Goldberg were so thrilled to get an opportunity to write an episode Seth guest-starred on. Everyone says, 'I can't believe I got to do it!' Someday we'll look at that picture of us recording and say, 'Remember that day we recorded *The Simpsons*?' That's *always* at the top of the list."

It's an Honor to Be Nominated . . . but a Bitch to Lose

The Simpsons has won thirty-two Emmys, more than any other sitcom except *Frasier*, which has thirty-seven. Each of our cast members has won at least one—Dan Castellaneta received four for playing Homer. Even our guest stars have won Emmys: Kelsey Grammer for Sideshow Bob, Jackie Mason as Rabbi Krustofsky, Marcia Wallace as Mrs. Krabappel, and Anne Hathaway as Krusty's sidekick Princess Penelope.

We've won ten Emmys for Outstanding Animated Program,

and even two for Outstanding Music and Lyrics: "We Put the Spring in Springfield" (1997) and "You're Checkin' In" (1998). Both songs were composed by *Simpsons* writer Ken Keeler, and they're both Broadway showstoppers with unconventional topics: one's about a whorehouse; the other's about a drug rehab clinic.

The Simpsons has won so many Emmys, it was parodied on the *Simpsons/Family Guy* crossover. Peter Griffin picks a fight with Homer Simpson. Homer yanks open an enormous cabinet stuffed with Emmys, which he hurls at Peter one by one.

Me and Joel Cohen, forty-five seconds after losing the 2017 Emmy.

Yet there are still people who think *The Simpsons* has never won an Emmy. That's because our awards aren't handed out at the boring televised ceremony. Our awards are handed out at the *super*-boring, untelevised ceremony, the Creative Arts Awards. This is a four-hour awards show honoring achievements in lighting, sound design, picture editing, hairstyling, makeup . . . and animation. It's a ceremony so dull, one year I watched the host—a popular TV comedian—wrap up the show, storm offstage, and immediately call his agent to say, "I am never ever going to do that show again."

In addition to Emmys, *The Simpsons* has won thirty Annie Awards for animation, eleven Writers Guild Awards for our scripts, and the first Peabody Award ever given to an animated

Tom Jones holds his *Simpsons* character design. With him *(left to right),* *Simpsons* writers: Al Jean, me (seventy pounds heavier), some guy, George Meyer, Jeff Martin. In front, three-foot-tall Conan O'Brien.

show. We've even won six Genesis Awards, and I don't know what the hell they are!

But we want more—awards are addictive. Sam Simon once crafted an elaborate mystery plot for the episode "Black Widower" hoping to win an Edgar Award from the Mystery Writers of America. He didn't get one—but I did, in 2000, for my caveman detective story "Cro-Magnon, P.I." The award is a painted plaster bust of Edgar Allan Poe; it looks like a novelty bottle that should be filled with bourbon, as the real Poe often was.

I think we've even got a shot at the Nobel Prize in Literature. If Bob Dylan's folk songs can win, why not Matt Groening's internationally beloved cartoon? My college pal Saul Perlmutter won the Nobel Prize in Physics, and he said the Nobels are a four-day party in Sweden. Sounds better than the Creative Arts Emmys.

I ♡ Celebrities

I know there are rotten celebrities out there. There's the lovable family comic (not Tim Allen) whom my friend called the worst man on earth. And the sitcom star (still not Tim Allen) who was so mean he made an Air Force colonel cry. And the lovable family comic/sitcom star who did two years in prison for selling coke (um . . .).

I've heard that Bruce Willis is so monstrous that one of his directors, a cancer survivor, said, "I'd go through another round of chemo rather than work with Bruce again."

I have no stories like this. All the celebrities I've worked with have two things in common: they're much smarter than you'd think, and they're incredibly nice.

Take **Rob Schneider**. I was hired to help him make a dumb movie script even dumber; when I asked him to describe the lead character, he went into a twenty-minute discourse on Jean-Jacques Rousseau's noble savage. Rob also cooked me French toast, something my mother never did.

There's nothing weird about **"Weird Al" Yankovic:** he's a solid family man and incredibly sweet. And another thing you probably don't know is that he skipped two grades in high school and graduated as class valedictorian.

Weird Al pitches a joke I don't like, outside Moe's Tavern, Universal Studios Hollywood.

And there's **Tom Arnold**. I assumed he was a dope and challenged him to a game of chess. He kicked my butt so bad (while simultaneously making a phone call and eating a plate of ribs) that I never played chess again.

Behold Tom Arnold whipping me at chess.

For years, I kept a typewritten fan letter on my office wall. It was the most cogent, articulate analysis of *The Simpsons* I'd ever read, so much so that I thought it belonged in a scholarly journal. The letter was signed "**Joey Ramone, the Ramones.**"

I worked with **Jim Carrey** on *Horton Hears a Who*. He was almost supernaturally kind—it was like writing gags for the Buddha. I witnessed one remarkable incident where he had to record the line "What?" (I wrote that!). He rattled off fifty-eight takes, all different, all funny. He told the recording engineer, "Play back take seventeen." The engineer played a take; Jim said, "That was take eighteen." He was right—the engineer then played back take seventeen, and it was the best of the bunch. Amazing.

David Copperfield called me out of the blue looking for a couple of jokes for his Vegas act. I don't even know how he got my number. (Magic?) I thought the whole thing was a prank; this must happen to him a lot, because he said, "After I hang up, go on YouTube and look at clips of me; you'll see it's the same voice." He not only became my friend, he's the greatest guy on earth (it's got to be someone)—funny, bright, charming, and generous.*

Of the 725 guest stars we've had on *The Simpsons,* I've heard complaints about only three: one actor, one author, one athlete. As for my personal experience, I've worked with only one celeb whom I considered a diva—I needed ten minutes of her time, but she'd only give me five. To protect her anonymity, the publisher's legal department will only let me give you her first name: **Oprah**.

---

* Here's what Copperfield says about ME: "What does it do to a person—all these years, all the Harvard stuff and *Carson* stuff and *Simpsons* stuff? All of that background informs the person Mike is, it teaches him what works and what doesn't, and gives him perspective. When this happens, you become a kind of sage. A comedy sage." Get a room, you guys.

Never visit the Statue of Liberty with David Copperfield—the man can't help himself.

BURNING QUESTION

Do you read what fans post on websites?

Yes. And it kills us. We have a lot of very loyal fans who seem to hate the show. Their website is even called NoHomers.net. This is like calling a Christian website JesusSucks.gov.

This website is the source of Comic Book Guy's catchphrase "Worst [BLANK] ever." Every Sunday, minutes after *The Simpsons* aired, some "fan" would post, "Worst episode ever." After weeks of this, someone posted at 8:15 P.M., "I'm halfway through tonight's show, but I can already tell it's the Worst Episode Ever!"

Then, one Tuesday night, someone posted, "I just saw the promo for next Sunday's *Simpsons,* and it clearly will be the Worst Episode Ever."

So why do these people keep watching the show? I stuck a fork in a light socket once and realized I should never do that again. These viewers keep sticking forks in the socket, week after week, year after year. And every time they're shocked that they're shocked (worst pun ever!).

Most of us rarely have the stomach to read the fan site. But as a diligent showrunner, Al Jean studies it every single week. Al Jean, whom the fans have said should "get cancer" or "die in a car crash." Why does he put himself through this? Because sometimes the fans get it right. They are especially sensitive when we write Homer too mean—a syndrome they call Jerk-Ass Homer. They say it and we listen.

But sometimes they should cut us some slack. One fan complained, "In Season 8, Homer smuggled beer. Then in Season 27, he smuggled snakes. Rip-off."

Yes, we did two vaguely similar stories, nineteen years apart. But the fan who complained was only fourteen years old—we hadn't even repeated ourselves in his lifetime!

Whatever the "fans" may say, people are still watching the show. Our ratings in season 29 were the highest they've been in years. To extrapolate from this, *The Simpsons* will run for five million years. But the fans will say it hasn't been funny since the three millionth season.

CHAPTER EIGHT

FOUR EPISODES THAT CHANGED THE WORLD (KINDA)

If you Google "Simpsons Best Episode List," you'll get 20,100,000 hits. If you Google "Simpsons Worst Episode List," you'll get 669,000 more (yeesh!). The point is, the world doesn't need another list of best episodes. Instead, I'd like to tell the never-before-told stories behind four *Simpsons* episodes I worked on that broke new ground and changed the series forever.

Seminal Episode Number 1: "Like Father Like Clown"

Often it takes just one joke to clinch an idea. This was the case with Jay Kogen and Wally Wolodarsky's "Like Father, Like Clown." It was a take on *The Jazz Singer*, with Krusty the Clown estranged from his Orthodox rabbi father. The problem was we'd never even said Krusty was Jewish in the show before. But then Al Jean pitched,

"His real name should be Krustofsky." It got a big laugh, particularly from Jim Brooks, and the idea was approved.

The show established a number of precedents:

1. **IT WAS ABOUT A PERIPHERAL CHARACTER.** Bart and Lisa save the day here, but it's Krusty's story, going all the way back to his childhood. Since then, we've explored almost every character's backstory, from Sideshow Mel's acting career to Carl's Icelandic roots. "Like Father, Like Clown" was a big revelation: *The Simpsons* doesn't have to be about the Simpsons.

2. **OTHER RELIGIONS ARE FUNNY, TOO.** This was only episode 41, but we'd already explored the family's religion, a Protestant sect called Presbylutheranism. But this show explored Judaism in a big way; in years to come, we'd tackle Homer's conversion to Catholicism, Apu's Hindu faith, and Lisa's embrace of Buddhism. We've made fun of every religion except Islam. There's nothing funny about those guys. Don't hurt us!

3. **HOMEWORK PAYS OFF.** The episode ends with a Talmudic debate between Rabbi Krustofsky and Bart. To write this, we enlisted the help of three real rabbis, as consultants. It remains the most scholarly debate you'll ever see on the nature of comedy and Judaism. In a cartoon. On Fox. Jay and Wally wrote a terrific script; it was beautifully animated by Brad Bird. And Jackie Mason, a former rabbi himself, was unexpectedly moving as Rabbi Krustofsky—he won an Emmy for the role.

We also learned another lesson—if you want to make a touching TV show, rip off a touching movie. *The Jazz Singer* has been remade several times—starring, respectively, Al Jolson, Danny Thomas, Jerry Lewis, and Neil Diamond. (It gets worse and worse!) It has always been a lousy movie, and yet the ending—where the rabbi reconciles with his entertainer son—always works.

It worked for us, too. The day after it aired, editorials praised the show. The Fox switchboard was flooded with calls: one man said it moved him to contact his father for the first time in twenty-five years. It was then that we realized our fans truly cared about our characters—all of our characters.

Except Lenny.

Seminal Episode Number 2: "Homer at the Bat"

"Homer at the Bat" changed the tone, the casting, the very reality of the show. It also saved a young boy's life. Really! What more could you ask for? Homer getting into the National Baseball Hall of Fame? Yeah, that happened, too.

It began when Sam Simon called Al Jean and me into his office to pitch a new story. Sam would explain an episode the way Oliver Hardy would lay out a scheme to Stan Laurel—in tiny, singsongy chunks, with long pauses in between. "Mr. Burns . . . is going to have . . . a softball team! And he'll hire nine ringers . . . to play on it! And we'll get nine professional ballplayers . . . to play themselves!"

This was season 3 of the show, and the previous seventeen episodes had covered baseball, mini golf, boxing, soapbox racing, and football. Now we were doing baseball *again*. As might be expected from a show written primarily by single men, *The Simpsons* was sports mad. For three months of every year, our office became a football pool that occasionally put out a TV show.

We even had our own bookie.

Everyone on staff loved sports . . . except me. But I served a

Homer is inducted into the Baseball Hall of Fame. Seated behind are Wade Boggs, Ozzie Smith, and Steve Sax from "Homer at the Bat."

purpose—I represented everyone's wives and mothers in the audience. I'd be the lone voice saying, "Will everyone get this joke about Mordecai 'Three Finger' Brown?" Yes, I was the Staff Girl. (To this day, I don't understand the ending of this episode—Homer wins the big game by getting knocked out cold by a pitch. How? Why? Huh? So what?)

Virtually any other *Simpsons* writer could have done this script. Jeff Martin and Jon Vitti had both worked as sportswriters. Al Jean would be the first person every year to buy the latest *Bill James Baseball Abstract;* by the following day, he had read and memorized the thousand-page doorstop.

But John Swartzwelder was our biggest baseball fan. He owns a huge amount of sports memorabilia, including what he claims is "the first baseball," which I imagine is made of mastodon hide and autographed by Ruth—not Babe, but the babe from the Old Testament.

We cast nine real-life baseball players (only Rickey Henderson and Ryne Sandberg turned us down), and Swartzwelder created quick, crazy stories for each of them:

- Ozzie Smith visits the Springfield Mystery Spot and plunges into a bottomless pit.
- Roger Clemens gets hypnotized and thinks he's a chicken.
- Wade Boggs gets into a fistfight over who was a better British prime minister, Lord Palmerston or Pitt the Elder.
- Ken Griffey Jr. overdoses on nerve tonic and gets gigantism. (Is that even a thing?)
- José Canseco does something nice for someone. (This one really stretched credibility.)

Up to this point, *The Simpsons* had been praised for its authenticity: "They're realer than most real families on TV," opined many a blowhard. But this episode didn't just stretch reality, it snapped it, hacked it to pieces, and left it to die in a drainage ditch. It was a very different *Simpsons* episode, including the fact that the Simpsons are barely in it. Here, the guest stars were running the asylum.

Needless to say, our cast didn't like the show. Our table reading of the script bombed utterly. Two of our actors complained about the script, the only time this has ever happened.

The baseball players were much easier to deal with. Don Mattingly had the only gripe: his character makes his first appearance wearing an apron and washing dishes. "Do I have to do this?" he moaned.

"I'm sorry, it's in the script, it can't be changed," Al Jean lied.

"Okay," Mattingly grumbled.

The players were surprisingly good actors. Mike Scioscia could be a real professional; in voice acting, you never know who's going to have the gift. (When Aerosmith did our show, their bass player Tom Hamilton had great comic timing and a huge range of funny voices.)

And then there was Ken Griffey Jr. He got angry because he didn't understand his line "There's a party in my mouth and everyone's invited." (If he had understood it, he'd have been *really* angry.) Adding to the pressure, his father, Ken Griffey Sr., was there trying to coach him through the line, and it wasn't helping.

The room was going to implode, so that's when they called in me, the Staff Girl. Since I didn't really know who Griffey was, they figured I wouldn't be intimidated by him. Al shoved me into the tiny recording booth. This instantly became my new worst fear: to be locked in a small glass booth with a large angry man; and I couldn't get out until I made him say a vaguely homoerotic line.

It took a few takes, but we got the line. Decades later, Griffey appeared in a mockumentary about the episode—he's become a much better actor.

Despite the misgivings of the cast, "Homer at the Bat" was a huge hit. It was the first time we beat our competition, *The Cosby Show*. We beat Cosby several more times after that; within two years his show was off the air.

It's also the show that intoxicated us with guest stars, and helped us realize we could get almost anyone we wanted. The next year, I insisted we do an all-star spectacular with celebrities I'd heard of: it was "Krusty Gets Kancelled," and it featured Elizabeth Taylor, Johnny Carson, Bette Midler, and many more. (Many more, but not Mandy Moore—I'm not a fan.)

"Homer at the Bat" also stretched the reality of the show, and nobody minded. The series would get a little crazier after that—

the next year we'd have Leonard Nimoy beam out of a scene like Mr. Spock. There was no turning back.

A quarter century has passed since "Homer at the Bat" debuted. Our bookie is long dead. We talk much less about sports and much more about tuition costs. Since 1992, our Staff Girl has been a real girl—currently, the brilliant Carolyn Omine.

But the episode is still remembered fondly. In May 2017, Homer was inducted into the National Baseball Hall of Fame. Wade Boggs, Steve Sax, and Ozzie Smith showed up at the ceremony. Smith said the number one question he gets asked is "How did you escape the Springfield Mystery Spot?" Boggs said he still sticks up for Pitt the Elder.

Oh yeah, and before I forget, the show really did save a kid's life. The episode opens with Homer choking on a doughnut; his friends ignore a prominently placed poster showing the Heimlich maneuver to study the sign-up sheet for Burns's softball team. A week later, the Los Angeles news featured an eight-year-old boy who saved his friend who was choking to death. When asked where he learned the Heimlich, he said, "It was on a poster on *The Simpsons*." True story.

And the name of the boy whose life was saved? It was Ryan Gosling.

That part's fake. I just needed an ending.

Seminal Episode Number 3: "Moaning Lisa"

In the first season, we were excited when our hero Jim Brooks wanted to pitch us an episode. His idea? Lisa is sad. That's it.

Jim would work out the details with us: Lisa is depressed and Marge can't help her. Then Lisa finds a jazz mentor in Bleeding Gums Murphy, who teaches her it's okay to be sad—and that cheers her up.

It didn't sound like a lot of fun, and it certainly didn't seem like a great use of animation. No one had much faith in the idea at the time. "Oh, you got stuck writing *that* one," Matt Groening said with a smirk.

"Jim's been trying to do this story since *Taxi*," Sam Simon told us. "Nobody would let him."

Jim's instinct was right, however, because this was the episode that cemented Lisa as a character. Up until then, she'd just been kind of a girl Bart. The first line we ever wrote for her was something she'd never say now: "Let's go throw rocks at the swans."

"Moaning Lisa" is the episode that first showed viewers the deep emotional reserves in *The Simpsons*, that a cartoon had the ability to move you, and even bum you out. Most of all, it showed that we weren't just a show for boys.

Since then, jazz has become a major element in our show. Not that any of us really like jazz.

I have always proudly thought, *There's never been a sitcom episode quite like "Moaning Lisa."* Then I watched a rerun of Jim Brooks's old series *The Mary Tyler Moore Show*—the plot of which is "Murray is sad." The episode even ends with Mary giving pretty much the same inspiring speech that Marge gives Lisa. But as Judd Apatow points out, "To me, a great *Simpsons* episode *should* feel like a great *Mary Tyler Moore*. There are some silly episodes, too, but I love the ones about people finding ways to connect with something larger. And *The Simpsons* has done this so many times in so many ways."

Six years later, Al and I pitched the sequel episode where Bleeding Gums dies. Ron Taylor, the lovable voice of Murphy (he looked exactly like the character) was at the cast reading of the script, and when we got to the point where he passes away, Ron shouted, "I'm dead?" He'd flown in from Colorado for the reading without ever looking at the script.

AL JEAN ON "MOANING LISA"

"People always tried to put labels on Mike and me. As a team, we were known as 'joke guys' on *The Tonight Show* or goofy shows like *ALF*. But when we got to *The Simpsons*, we wanted to do more emotional stories, like stories about Lisa, because we wanted to show we could do those kinds of things, too."

Seminal Episode Number 4: "Treehouse of Horror" (The First One)

The Simpsons' first season was a cultural phenomenon. Now, two episodes into the second season, we were doing a Halloween show, a trilogy of terror. It was a tremendously risky move. Just minutes into the show, we see a zombified Lisa, carrying a knife, about to murder her whole family. Maggie's head rotates like a lawn sprinkler.

It was so frightening that we opened the show with a disclaimer: Marge comes out from behind a stage curtain (aping an actual filmed preamble to the original *Frankenstein)* and warns the audience, "Tonight's show, which I totally wash my hands of, is really scary. So if you have sensitive children, maybe you should tuck them in early tonight, instead of writing us angry letters tomorrow."

The warning proved unnecessary: our fans loved the show. We did, too—how often do frustrated writers get to kill off their characters? A tradition was born.

The shows got bloodier and creepier every year, and no one complained. Nobody even cared when we showed it; if it aired anytime between September 12 and November 15, it was a Halloween show.

The show gets harder to write each year; by this point, we've had to come up with eighty-seven different horror archetypes. We quickly spoofed every horror film classic and all the great *Twilight Zone*s. Now we're parodying thrillers (*Dead Calm)*, great arthouse dramas (*The Diving Bell and the Butterfly*), lousy arthouse dramas (*Eyes Wide Shut)*, even Dr. Seuss. Lately—and this is really scary—we've had to come up with original stories! Make it stop!

It's even tougher on the animators: almost every segment has to be designed from scratch, drawing new characters, costumes, and sets. It's the first show we produce each season, which means we start the year by blowing out the budget and burning out the animators.

Even coming up with our own Halloween names for the credits has become a chore. I've been Murderous Mike Reiss, Macabre Mike Reiss, Dr. Michael & Mr. Reiss, Ms. Iris Eek (an anagram), The Thing from Bristol Connecticut, and The Abominable Dr. Reiss. (Hey, Dad—I finally became a doctor!)

We also learned one thing *not* to do from that first Halloween show: don't get pretentious. The third segment of that Treehouse of Horror was a retelling of "The Raven," starring Bart and Homer. It was literate, gorgeously animated . . . and boring. Edgar Allan Poe is a literary genius—my favorite author, in fact—but nobody ever called him funny. When we saw the finished animation, we realized we had to gag it up. We pieced together odd bits of animation to make new cutaway scenes where Bart makes fun of the poem. It helped, but it's still pretty stiff.

To this day, professors tell me how much they love that segment. Scholars cite it in academic papers. English teachers show it to their classes.

God, I'm so ashamed.

Special Mention:
"Homer and Lisa Exchange Cross Words"

The *Simpsons* writers love puzzles. As early as our first season, we had Bart anagramming a restaurant sign, changing COD PLATTER to COLD PET RAT.

Two decades later, we built an entire episode around puzzles, in our *Da Vinci Code* parody "Gone Maggie Gone": Maggie is kidnapped (by nuns!) and Lisa must solve a series of riddles to find her. My contribution: Lisa must find "the biggest ring in Springfield." It's the letters R-I-N-G in the town's giant SPRINGFIELD sign.

Crossword puzzles are our writers' real addiction (well, that and Percocet). Many of us start our day with the *New York Times* crossword. Our newest addition to the staff, Megan Amram, actually constructed a puzzle for the *Times*. We have one writer who does nothing but solve crosswords all day long—apparently this is what we pay him for.

I used to do crosswords to get my mind off work, but nowadays you can't do a puzzle without encountering LISA, MOE, or APU. I recently did one where the clue was "San Francisco mass transit": the answer was BART. *Thank God*, I thought. *The puzzle constructor could have used a* Simpsons *clue, but didn't.* Then I got to the final entry: "What you might say if you can't solve this last clue." The answer was DOH.

D'oh indeed.

Worlds collided in this great episode, "Homer and Lisa Exchange Cross Words":

Lisa finds she has an aptitude for crossword puzzles; she enters Springfield's crossword tournament, where Homer, unforgivably, bets against her. To atone, Homer persuades crossword constructor Merl Reagle and editor Will Shortz (playing themselves) to create a special puzzle for the *New York Times;* buried in the clues and solution are Homer's heartfelt apologies to Lisa.

What makes the episode amazing is that the final puzzle Lisa solved in our Sunday-night episode was the same crossword that appeared in that morning's *New York Times*. Merl Reagle, a brilliant and funny man, had slipped an elaborate *Simpsons* message past millions of *Times* readers.

It's worth mentioning that the episode's author, Tim Long, is the rare *Simpsons* writer who doesn't give a crap about crossword puzzles. This happens a lot on our show. The Simpsons visit Israel in "The Greatest Story Ever D'ohed"—the Israeli people loved it, and the show was nominated for a Humanitas Award for its "promotion of human dignity." The episode was written by the rare non-Jew on our staff—Kevin Curran, a product of Catholic schools, who never set foot in Israel.

If you like puzzles half as much as we do, you might like these challenges I've created for Will Shortz on NPR's *Weekend Edition Sunday*. (Shortz always refers to me on the air as "former *Simpsons* writer Mike Reiss." Former? What has he heard that I haven't?) None of the puzzles involve *The Simpsons;* they're mostly about pop culture, and there's a few sneaky twists thrown in.*

1. Think of a two-word phrase you might see on a clothing label. Add two letters to the end of the first word, and one letter to the end of the second word. The result is the name of a famous writer. Who is it?

2. Name a well-known TV actress of the past. Put an R between her first and last names. Then read the result backward. The result will be an order Dr. Frankenstein might give to Igor. Who is the actress, and what is the order?

3. A famous actress and a famous director share the same

---

* Answers are on page 289. Feel free to cheat. Bart would.

last name, although they are unrelated. The first name of one of these is a classic musical. The first name of the other is an anagram of a classic musical. Who are they?

4. Take the first name of a famous actress. Drop a letter. Rearrange what's left, and you'll get a word used in a particular sport. This actress's last name, without any changes, is where that sport is played. What actress is it?

5. Take the name of a well-known actress. Her first name starts with the three-letter abbreviation for a month. Replace this with the three-letter abbreviation of a different month, and you'll get the name of a famous poet. Who are these two people?

6. Name a famous Greek person from history. Rearrange the letters of the name to get the title of a famous Italian person from history. Who are these two people?

7. Name a famous actress whose last name ends in a doubled letter. Drop that doubled letter. Then insert an R somewhere inside the first name. The result will be a common two-word phrase. What is it?

8. Take two words that go together to make a familiar phrase in this form: "blank and blank." Both words are plurals, such as "bells and whistles." Move the first letter of the second word to the start of the first word. You'll get two new words that name forms of transportation. What are they?

9. Take the two-word title of a TV series. The first word contains a famous actor's first name in consecutive letters. The second word is a homophone for this actor's last name. Name the series and the actor.

The alien lineup from our *X-Files* crossover show "The Springfield Files": Marvin the Martian from *Looney Tunes*, Gort from *The Day the Earth Stood Still*, Chewbacca, ALF, and Kang (or Kodos—who can tell?). Al Jean called it "the most illegal shot in *Simpsons* history": not only didn't we get permission to use these characters, we even had Dan Castellaneta say "Yo!" as ALF. The only complaint we got was from Paul Fusco, the creator and voice of the puppet. He said, "Next time you put ALF on the show, let me do the voice!"

10. Take the phrase "no sweat." Using only these seven letters, and repeating them as often as necessary, can you make a familiar four-word phrase? It's fifteen letters long. What is it?

11. Name an occupation in nine letters. It's an entertainer of sorts—an unusual and uncommon but well-known sort of entertainer. Drop the third letter of the name, and read the result backward. You'll get two four-letter words that are exact opposites. What are they?

12. Think of a ten-letter occupation ending in *-er*. The first four letters can be rearranged to spell something that a person would study, and the next four letters can be rearranged to spell something else that person would study. What is the occupation?

13.   What six-letter word beginning with the letter *s* would be the same if it started with *th*?

Homer's Massive Boners

I have only a few regrets about my career, and one of them is titling this section with a boner joke. We have a pretty good sense of what our audience can handle; if you're easily offended, you probably stopped watching back in 1990. There are only four things we've done in the show's history that I wish we could do over:

1.   **BART'S TOURETTE'S:** We wrote a scene where, to get out of taking a test, Bart pretended to have Tourette syndrome. The censors had no problem with this, but thousands of viewers did; it's the most complaints we ever got about one joke. When the show reran, we changed Bart's ailment from Tourette syndrome to rabies, the one time we've ever altered a line after public outcry. Rabies is still pretty bad, but if you pet a foaming dog, it's your fault.

2.   **NEW ORLEANS:** We did a musical parody of *A Streetcar Named Desire* that opened with a song making fun of New Orleans. Some of the writers were skittish, but I said, "People in New Orleans have a great sense of humor—they're going to love it."
      Well, they don't and they didn't.
      The song began, "New Orleans—home of pirates, drunks, and whores!" That didn't bother them—that's

on their license plates. But the next line of the couplet was "New Orleans—tacky overpriced souvenir stores!" That's what pissed them off.

The local Fox affiliate, owned by Quincy Jones, yanked the show off the air for two weeks. To make matters worse, Bart was supposed to be King of Carnival at Mardi Gras that year. A New Orleans reporter called to tell me, "When your friend Bart comes down here . . . we're gonna kill him."

I said, "Well, you know, it's not really going to be Bart. It'll be a tiny man in a foam rubber suit."

The reporter replied, "Well then, we're gonna kill him."

They probably did.

3. **ADOPTING LISA:** We were doing an episode where Homer's having a triple bypass and we'd written ourselves into a corner: how does a father say goodbye to his kids, knowing he might die during surgery?

"Oh, that's easy," said Jim Brooks, and he pitched a scene off the top of his head: Lisa whispers to Homer all the things he needs to tell Bart; then Bart does the same for Lisa.

It was clever, funny, and exceptionally moving. Except for one line. Jim Brooks had Bart telling Lisa, "I guess this is the time to tell you . . . you're adopted and I never liked you."

Many parents of adopted children complained that this is their kids' worst nightmare.

A decade later, my friend was developing a sitcom about a girl who feels she doesn't fit in with her family. She said, "We're calling it *Maybe I'm Adopted*."

"No, you're not," I said. "You'll never get away with it."

"Oh, I will," my friend said. "The network loves the title."

When the show eventually came on, it was called *Maybe It's Me*.

4. **KILLING MAUDE**: I left *The Simpsons* for two years to pursue my own projects. When I returned, in 2000, we were working on a Ned Flanders scene and I pitched a line for his wife, Maude. Everyone looked around guiltily, and writer Ian Maxtone-Graham finally admitted, "We killed her." Why? Because the actress who played her asked for a raise.

Maude died in the 1999 episode "Alone Again, Natura-Diddily"—she was shot in the face with a T-shirt cannon and knocked over the back wall of an auto speedway. Some critics liked the episode, but it also received the full spectrum of knocks, from "harsh and cynical" to "sappy and lame." One critic even said, "Killing Maude was a sin." I have to agree with that: we killed the nice wife of a nice guy, leaving his two nice but annoying kids motherless.

When we make a big change like this—Apu having octuplets, Patty and Selma adopting a baby—we always think we'll get some great episodes out of it. We rarely do.

A few years later, we were doing a show where Krusty gets bar mitzvahed; the episode was supposed to begin with Krusty's father, Rabbi Krustofsky, dying. Finally, someone asked, "Why are we killing off all our great characters? The bloodshed must stop!"

Krusty's father was spared.

We killed him ten years later.

BEST EPISODES EVER (IN MY HUMBLE OPINION, WHICH IS BETTER THAN YOURS)

"Marge vs. the Monorail" (season 4): Conan O'Brien came in with this story on his first day at *The Simpsons*. Script by Conan, directed by Oscar winner Rich *"Zootopia"* Moore: no wonder it's a classic.

"The Father, the Son, and the Holy Guest Star" (season 16): Homer becomes a Catholic—why did it take us sixteen years to hit on this idea? And here's a line you don't hear often: Liam Neeson was hilarious.

"Radio Bart" (season 3): Matt Groening pitched this great story where Bart falls down a well. Terrific direction, Sting duets with Krusty—we lost our first Emmy Award with this.

"The Seemingly Never-Ending Story" (season 17): A story within a story within a story . . . within a story! You don't get that on *SpongeBob*.

"Treehouse of Horror VI" (season 7): For years, one segment of every Halloween show kinda sucked. We usually stuck it in the middle. Treehouse VI was the first to have three great segments. Plus 3-D Homer! And Paul Anka!

"Simpsoncalifragilisticexpiala(AnnoyedGrunt)cious" (season 8): Al Jean always wanted to do a *Mary Poppins* parody. I fought him on this for five years—thank God I lost. It's the most popular thing we ever wrote together.

"King-Size Homer" (season 7): Fat Homer is funny. Really fat Homer is really funny. Look at Peter Griffin.

"Lisa the Skeptic" (season 9): There are only two seasons of *Simpsons* episodes I didn't work on, and I'm afraid the show is smarter and funnier without me. This one is my favorite.

"Last Exit to Springfield" (season 4): I told Jay Kogen, who co-wrote this with Wally Wolodarsky, that *USA Today* had named it the best *Simpsons* episode ever. He laughed. "It wasn't even the best one we wrote that month."

WORST EPISODES—EVER!

"Breitbart/Dumb Bart" (season 27): To impress Milhouse, Bart says that Homer sells nuclear secrets. Calling Milhouse a "high-level source," this fake news makes it to Breitbart, and ultimately the White House. Homer is sent to Guantanamo, where he goes on a hunger strike. It lasts fifteen minutes.

"Seoul Train!" (season 12): The Simpsons are going to South Korea! They visit an animation house, never realizing it's the one where they themselves are animated. Bart befriends the other ten-year-olds who work in the studio and convinces them to quit. Also, Maggie crosses into North Korea and launches a missile.

"The Simpsons/SpongeBob Crossover Spectacular" (season 8): After Mr. Burns dumps toxic waste in Springfield Harbor, the whole cast of *SpongeBob SquarePants* is forced to move in with the Simpsons. Marge immediately warms to Bob as "the best kitchen sponge I ever used."

"King of the Hillary" (season 28): Severely misjudging the political climate, the *Simpsons* writers produced this Inauguration Day-special where Trump lost the election. The show features Lisa and Bill Clinton playing the sax at Hillary's inaugural ball, while an embittered Trump becomes Grampa's new roommate at Springfield Retirement Castle.

"World Cup Sucker" (season 15): Homer reads an obviously fake list of Krusty's Worst Episodes Ever—and falls for it. What a moron!

BURNING QUESTION

What do you think of *Family Guy*?

I get this question every time I make a public appearance. No one ever asks my opinion on *Archer* (overrated), *South Park* (same show every week), or *BoJack Horseman* (never seen it).

When *Family Guy* debuted ten years into *The Simpsons'* run, our younger writers were incensed: "It's just vulgar!" "It moves too fast!" "It's nothing but pop culture references!"

I had to laugh, because these were all things people said about *The Simpsons* when it began. Maybe that's why I have a soft spot for *Family Guy*: I think of it as *The Simpsons* after a few beers. As opposed to *Adventure Time*, which is like *The Simpsons* after a series of small strokes.

Our staff would complain endlessly about *Family Guy*, managing to hold two completely contradictory opinions: "It's exactly like our show!" and "They do things we'd never do!" The latter is where the show's charm lies. I'm a jaded, old TV writer, but that show somehow manages to shock me on a weekly basis. They do jokes about

AIDS, abortion, and the Holocaust, topics we've never touched.

Family Guy creator Seth MacFarlane is like our Ned Flanders: no matter how much we berate him, he's always warm and gracious (and the first to admit his debt to our show). Clearly, this is a man who looked at Homer Simpson and said, "He needs to be bigger and dumber."

We're all family. We boost each other's ratings, and make Fox Sunday night a viewer destination. Even the writing staffs have begun to blend: *Simpsons* showrunner Mike Scully's brother now writes for *Family Guy; Simpsons* alum Rich Appel runs the show.

All this crossbreeding made the unthinkable a reality: a *Simpsons/Family Guy* crossover show. When Matt Groening and Jim Brooks agreed to this, I imagined they'd oversee every aspect of the episode. Instead, amazingly, they told *Family Guy,* "Good luck with the crossover. We'll watch it when it airs." In the end, everyone from both camps loved it . . . except maybe Seth MacFarlane. The running theme of the episode was that *Family Guy* stole everything from *The Simpsons.* They made this point over and over and over and over. Apparently, at some point Seth told his staff, "Guys—enough."

I'll close with a story you may know, and which I heard from Seth himself. Years ago, he spent a weekend in Boston but had to catch a plane back to L.A. His travel agent gave him the wrong time, and he arrived just as his plane took off without him. Seth got on the phone and was yelling at his travel agent when he looked up at an airport TV—the plane he was supposed to be on had just crashed into the World Trade Center.

What's the point of this story? The point is that I like *Family Guy* . . . but God friggin' loves *Family Guy*!

CHAPTER NINE

MEET THE FANS

One of the great perks of working at *The Simpsons* is that I get to travel the world talking about it. I have a lecture that's filled with secrets, scandals, and flat-out lies (just like this book!) that's called "The Simpsons Backstage Tour." (That's another one of those jokes no one gets: there is no backstage at an animated show.) My first lecture was in 2000—since then, I've brought it to four hundred venues in thirty-six U.S. states and twenty-one foreign countries. (You can book me through Gotham Artists—ADV.)

Since we don't have a studio audience, these personal appearances are the one chance I get to interact with our fans. They are so sweet and appreciative of all the hard work we do. It's a wonderful change of pace from the handful of angry trolls who attack us on *Simpsons* websites. In fact, several times, the gushiest fans I've met admit to me, "I'm one of those assholes on NoHomers.net." I love these guys.

I've learned a lot from them over the years, including many surprises. For example, when I ask about their favorite characters, I often don't hear them say Bart or Homer. I hear Duffman and Disco Stu instead.

Duffman started as a one-shot character, and Disco Stu was a typo on a denim jacket. (It was supposed to read "Disco Stud.") But because of this feedback, we've featured them both on the show many times since.

Importantly, the fans helped resurrect Ralph. I'll admit it, around season 4 we were getting tired of the little weirdo. His inspired lines, like "My cat's breath smells like cat food," were getting harder to write and formulaic. So we simply stopped writing for him, and he only appeared once or twice a year. But when I visited college campuses, I observed how he was the most imitated and most quoted of all our characters. When I told the other writers about this, they brought Ralph back from exile. A decade later, he would open *The Simpsons Movie:* he's the first character you see, appearing in the Fox logo.

Another big thing I've learned from my lectures is that *Simpsons* fans are cool—there's not a Comic Book Guy in the bunch. The best part of my presentation is the Q&A (the most-asked Q's make up the Burning Question sections of this book), and the questions are always smart and never too geeky. Except this one:

"In season 4, Moe said he had small ears. In season 8, he said he had big ears. How can this be?"

The crowds are surprisingly well behaved, too. Frat boys in the south are always polite; it's financial services executives who are out of control. (I don't know why, but I'm always asked to speak at their conventions.) These guys are generally drunk, and they tend to heckle. They're not even good at it—one guy kept yelling *"Animal House!"* throughout my lecture. These are the people who are handling your pension fund.

Another thing I learned is that what you say on campus does not stay on campus. I gave a speech at North Dakota State University in Fargo (jealous?). That night, I got an angry call from the president of Fox, who said, "You can't go around North Dakota badmouthing the network."

I said, "I don't think I badmouthed it . . ."

"You compared the Fox network to a sewer," she said.

I replied, "Not in a bad way."

The biggest crowd I ever played to was two thousand people at Florida State University. They told me they hired five bodyguards to protect me—three uniformed, two undercover. I told them I'd never needed a bodyguard in my life.

They admitted, "Well, we had Gorbachev speak here last week, and we still had the bodyguards on payroll."

That night, a nut rushed the stage during my talk to pitch me some episode ideas. I yelled for my bodyguards, but no one came; they were all smoking in the alley.

I have a special speech that focuses on Judaism and the series, called "The Simpsons and Other Jewish Families." It focuses on Krusty, Rabbi Krustofsky, and the Simpson family trip to Israel. I've given it at dozens of synagogues, Jewish film festivals, and charity events all over the world. The toughest act I ever had to follow was at a Jewish fund-raiser in Toronto. They opened by showing a film featuring newsreel footage of the Holocaust and terrorism in Israel; the film ended with a picture of Anne Frank and the quote "Hope is a dying ember in our world." The movie ended, the lights came up, and everyone in the audience was racked with sobs. And then the rabbi said, "And now the comedy of Mike Reiss!"

The best audience I ever had was at another Jewish event, the New Hampshire Jewish Film Festival. My audience consisted of every Jewish senior citizen in Manchester, New Hampshire. These people had clearly never seen *The Simpsons,* since they were circulating a cheat sheet one of their grandsons had made about the show. It featured such facts as "Homer Simpson works in a barbershop."

"This is wrong," I told one elderly Shebrew.

"My grandson is never wrong," she replied.

I expected a disaster, and yet this was the sharpest group I ever had. They laughed at every joke, often before I finished it.

There must be something in the water in New Hampshire: there's only ten thousand Jews in the state, but three of them are Seth Meyers, Adam Sandler, and Sarah Silverman.

Believe me, not all my lectures go that well. I gave the commencement address at a girls' school in South Carolina. There were seven hundred people in the audience. I could hear five hundred people laughing; what I couldn't hear was the other two hundred people silently hating my guts. When the speech ended, I thought I'd done well, until a phalanx of student security guards surrounded me. "We have to get you out of here," one guard whispered. "There are people in this audience who want to kill you."

What had I done to make them so mad? I'd made a joke about then-president George W. Bush, whom I'd called "Satan with a learning disorder." Mind you, this was 2008—the U.S. economy had just collapsed, and Bush's approval rating stood at around 9 percent. I guess all 9 percent were sitting in my audience.

Was the Bush joke offensive? It certainly offended them, but the rest of the audience loved it. And it's my belief that a joke is only in bad taste if it doesn't get a laugh. Take Anne Frank—as I learned at my Toronto speech, there's nothing funny about her tragic story. Except that there's a classic joke that's so funny it overcomes our sensitivities:

> Brooke Shields was so bad in a production of *The Diary of Anne Frank* that when the Nazis came onstage, the audience yelled, "She's in the attic!"

I had this epiphany about bad taste in 2017, when blogger Milo Yiannopoulos was mired in controversy for his sexist, racist, homophobic blogging. It was only when I saw this smirking boob on *Real Time with Bill Maher* that I realized, *Oh my God, he thinks he's funny.* Joan Rivers made the same kind of jokes as Milo—she called Michelle Obama "Blackie-O"—but her jokes were funny, and Milo's weren't.

I had another realization after my South Carolina speech: a sense of humor isn't the ability to laugh at other people; it's the ability to laugh at yourself. I tried to explain this to a disgruntled audience member at another lecture, where I told the true story about a children's book I wrote being banned in Texas. A woman accosted me after the show and said, "I'm from Texas, and I didn't appreciate your making fun of it."

"I also made jokes about Jews, homosexuals, Arkansas, pedophilia, Woody Allen, the French, and myself," I replied. "Did you have any problem with those?"

"No, those were fine."

"So any joke is okay, as long as it's not about you?"

"Mr. Rice," she said, indignantly mispronouncing my name, "you don't burn brighter by blowing out someone else's candle."

"Well, you kinda do," I said.

DAVID COPPERFIELD ON MY SPEECHES

"I'm a very apt pupil and audience for all things Mike Reiss. I'm the one who gets sent all the videos of him on vacation and traveling around. They're really, really funny. Some of them you can't air. But I love them. They make me laugh. He sends me his latest speeches, too. People don't think of me as a joke-teller, but there's tons of comedy in my show. So Mike tells me about troubles he might have with his latest audience, because I suppose he thinks he can commiserate with a fellow person who's 'up there' telling jokes."

Worst Speech Ever

That South Carolina audience wanted to murder me, but I've had worse crowds. I gave a speech about *The Simpsons* just days after 9/11. No one felt much like laughing, particularly since the event was being held at the World Trade Centre of Hong Kong.

The man who'd booked me for the event was a big *Simpsons* fan; his audience wasn't. They were all native Chinese: they had never seen *The Simpsons,* and they barely understood English. I sweated through my one-hour speech, and got exactly one laugh: when I used the word "Viagra" (bless that word!). After the speech, my host said, "I've never seen a Chinese audience laugh that much."

That single laugh was one laugh more than I got with that same speech at a college in the south. It doesn't matter which one—it was an Arkansas state university.

My plane arrived in Mississippi—the closest airport wasn't even in the same state. My host introduced himself as Professor Eisenberg from New Jersey.

"What's a Jewish guy from Jersey doing teaching in Arkansas?" I asked.

He sighed rabbinically. "Sometimes you take the hand life deals you." He went silent for the next two hours of the drive.

When I arrived at the campus, the lecture hall was filling up nicely. A young student said, "I can't believe so many people showed up on a Wednesday."

"What happens on Wednesday?" I asked.

"Church night!" she snapped contemptuously. Then she asked if I needed anything.

"Just some water," I said. It's the one demand in my contract—a glass of water.

She rolled her eyes like I was Queen of the Divas and sulked off. She returned with a bottle of water and slammed it on my lectern.

I went into my speech and didn't get one laugh. Not even on "Viagra." Uh-oh. My mouth went dry, so I opened my bottle of hard-won water. It was frozen solid. It was ice and so was my audience.

Even when my speech goes badly, I can usually redeem myself with the Q&A—it's the liveliest part of my presentation. "Any questions?" I asked.

None. These Arkansas students apparently knew everything about animation, TV production, and comedy. They shuffled out grimly, clearly thinking, *I missed church night for this?*

After the speech, Professor Eisenberg took me to a restaurant with his two young sons. And then he vanished for a couple of hours, leaving me with his kids. Clearly, since I'd failed as a speaker, he decided to use me as a babysitter.

Occasionally, when I tell this story, someone says, "I'm from Arkansas, and we don't act like that."

I tell them this was Jonesboro, Arkansas.

"Oh," they reply. "Never mind."

The Bermuda Triangle of Radio Stations

I was booked to give a speech in Bermuda, and the sponsor said they needed help selling tickets.

"Selling?" I asked. "People usually get to see my show for free." The sponsor told me the tickets were going for fifty-five dollars—and they weren't going fast. Folks, I give a pretty good lecture, but it wouldn't be worth fifty-five bucks if I threw in an oil change.

To promote my appearance, they'd booked me on a local jazz radio station on Saturday at nine A.M. "No one in Bermuda is awake at nine on a Saturday morning," I said. "Especially jazz fans."

My sponsor assured me that it was a very popular radio show, and the DJ told me that he was a "big, big *Simpsons* fan." I got on the air with him. "We're givin' away two free tickets to Mike Reiss's show," he said. "So, Mike, give me a trivia question for our viewers to answer. Make it a hard one!"

"All right," I said. "What was the name of Bart's pet elephant?" (Answer: Stampy)

"Our phone lines are open!" said the DJ. And they stayed open. Not one call came in for the next twenty minutes.

Finally, the DJ said, "Maybe that question was a little too hard. Give 'em an easier one!"

"All right—what is the name of Bart Simpson's dog?" (Answer: Santa's Little Helper)

The phones remained silent for another twenty minutes. The laid-back DJ was getting upset—I'd never seen a stressed-out Rasta before. "Mike, your questions are too hard! Give the audience a real easy one!"

"Fine," I said. "What is the name of Bart Simpson's father?"

It was another ten minutes before the phone mercifully rang. The DJ listened to the caller, then turned to me. "He says it's 'Santa's Little Helper.' Is that the name of Bart's father?" This was the same DJ who'd told me he was a "big, big *Simpsons* fan."

Unsurprisingly, I didn't get a big crowd that night in Bermuda. But I assured the few who came that they'd have some laughs. Then I told the tech crew to play the reel of *Simpsons* clips I'd brought along. Instead, on the big screen overhead, there appeared an ad for Friskies Buffet. These people had paid fifty-five bucks apiece to see a cat food commercial. After the ad, the video screen went to an old episode of *Seinfeld*. The tech crew couldn't seem to turn it off, so the audience and I just watched the whole show. It was a good one, too: the yada-yada-yada episode.

"See," I said to the audience. "I told you you'd have some laughs."

Wrong Professor Theories . . .

A professor at a prestigious university once wrote to me and said, "I teach *The Simpsons* in my poli-sci class. Would you address my students? I've attached my notes to prepare you."

I wrote back, "I'd love to address your class, but I'll have to say that everything you're teaching them is wrong."

He sent back a two-word reply: "DON'T COME."

Which is the first time I heard that. From a *man*.

This was not a unique case. They now teach entire courses on *The Simpsons* at many colleges. I think this is an excellent sign. Of the apocalypse.

I don't mind that they're teaching *The Simpsons*. What bothers me is that they're getting it all wrong. And if they're getting *The Simpsons* wrong, what are the odds they're getting physics right?

For example, I was lecturing at a prestigious university, and a professor introduced me with a long discourse on why we named our hero Homer: clearly, the character was on an epic journey through life, like the sagas written by the Greek poet Homer.

It's a beautiful theory, except for the fact that it's 100 percent wrong. Matt Groening really did just name the character after his dad. Like almost everything we do, there wasn't much thought put into it.

I met a professor of humor studies (that's a real thing) at another university. He expounded on his philosophy of what made *The Simpsons* funny. As he nattered on, I thought, *If I were to sculpt a man out of pure shit, he would not be as full of shit as this professor.*

Worst of all, professors never back down. I attended a Slovakian animation festival where the grand prize winner was a student film called "Pandas." The young director said in his acceptance speech, "My teacher gave me a C+ on this!" I met his teacher and told her that "Pandas" was the greatest cartoon I'd seen in my life—epic in scale and filled with brilliant jokes. The teacher stood her ground, saying, "I should have given it a C–."

I've worked on *The Simpsons* for thirty years, and I've never thought too deeply about it, but scholars insist on analyzing our show. There's a website called Simpsons Archive that collects academic papers about *The Simpsons*. I once spent a day scanning through them, thinking, *Wrong. Wrong. Wrong.* Two basic mistakes pop up over and over. One is that if we parody something, we must hate it: parody equals contempt. That's ridiculous—Al and I have parodied nearly every scene in Orson Welles' *Citizen Kane* because we love the film and know it inside out. (We've parodied Orson himself because he was a big fat whale.)

The bigger mistake is thinking that there's an overarching philosophy to the series. There isn't. The show is written by a diverse and ever-changing group of people, and each episode stands on its own.

If the show has a philosophy, it's "We don't have a philosophy." Take the Halloween segment where Lisa wishes for world peace. Mankind destroys all the weapons, only to be conquered by an alien with a slingshot. "Foolish earthlings," intones Kang, "your superior intellects are no match for our puny weapons."

What's our point? Weapons are good? World peace is bad? We work very hard to have no point. As Homer says at the end of the 1991 episode "Blood Feud," "Maybe it's just a bunch of stuff that happened."

. . . And Flat-Out Nutty Fan Theories

Most academic theories of *The Simpsons* are wrong and boring. I much prefer the fan theories: they're wrong and *crazy*. Take the student who asked me at one lecture, "Does Ned Flanders have superpowers? The internet says he does because in last week's episode, he was looking through a wall."

"That was a window," I explained.

Another fan theory on the net states that after Homer went into a coma in one season 4 episode, he never woke up. The subsequent twenty-six seasons have all been a dream. This theory is not so much science as religion: a cool story with absolutely nothing to back it up.

The most bizarre theory was inspired by our 1997 episode "The City of New York vs. Homer Simpson," which takes place almost entirely at the World Trade Center. After the 9/11 attacks, this show was pulled from syndication for several years. The episode features a brochure for a nine-dollar tour of New York and a picture of the WTC—and the numeral 9 next to the Twin Towers looks sort of like "9 11."

This gave rise to the incredible conspiracy theory that the *Simpsons* writers are all members of Skull and Bones—even though that's a Yale organization, and we're largely Harvard grads, without a single Yalie on staff. The theory continues that we were all recruited from Skull and Bones to join the CIA, and four years before the 9/11 attacks, we decided to leak our complicity in the conspiracy in an episode of our show.

Let me put these conspiracy rumors to rest once and for all: they're completely true.

BURNING QUESTION

What do you say to people who say the show has gone downhill?

I love this question because no one ever asks, "Why has the show gone downhill?" It's always, "*What do you say* to people who say the show has gone downhill?"

You're not fooling me. I'm still offended. It's like asking, "I'm not saying your sister's a slut . . . but *what do you say* to the hundreds of guys who say she is?"

Here are the facts: TV shows age like people, and each episode is like a birthday. Many shows die in infancy. You can syndicate a show after seventy-two episodes—just like seventy-two years is the average life expectancy for an American man. When a show makes it to one hundred episodes, or a person makes it to a hundred years, that's cause for celebration.

Our show is a 658-year-old man. And you're asking why it's not as cute as it used to be? We're lucky *The Simpsons* can still pee.

There's another way shows age like people: when they get old, they get either weird or boring. Those are your only two choices. By the end of its run, *M*A*S*H* got boring. *Seinfeld* got weird. *Cosby* got boring, but Cosby himself got weird.

We've opted for weird. We do two to three plot lines per episode, which means after three decades, we've burned through nearly two thousand stories. To do a new episode, we have to think of the two-thousand-and-first best idea out there. We've run through all the normal ones—every Simpsons family member has had a crush on someone, or had someone get a crush on them. We've killed off seven recurring characters—in one background shot, we showed a graveyard filled with dead characters.

At least we hope we're never boring. The pace of our show gets faster all the time. And since the show went hi-def in 2009, we jam more jokes into the background that you couldn't have seen before. Recently Lisa was in a library, and we had to come up with thirty funny titles for the books behind her. She's not going back to the library anytime soon.

AL JEAN ON QUALITY

"It's hard for me to be objective about the show and what era is better. But I will say you can't say we didn't try hard, work hard, and last a long time. We always go up from 'lead-ins,' and whatever show follows us goes down, which is a sign that people are watching you just for you. I don't know when it will end; there are factors of cost. All I can say is we really care about it like it's a show that's just starting out. We've never lost that feeling."

CHAPTER TEN

SEEING THE WORLD WITH
THE SIMPSONS

I've visited 113 countries. Not by choice. My travel tastes range from Disneyland to Disneyworld.

But my wife loves to travel. We've been to the North Pole and the South Pole—if they ever find an East Pole, I'm sure we'll be going there. My wife has even dragged her clearly Semitic husband to every Jew-hating place on earth: Iran, Iraq, Syria, South Carolina. So why do I go? Because I fear my wife more than I fear ISIS.

I'm always on the move—portions of the book you're holding were written in Kazakhstan, Uzbekistan, Egypt, Japan, and Epcot Center; I'm typing this sentence in a Sudanese city called "Wow!" You may travel to forget about work, but I don't have that luxury because people watch *The Simpsons everywhere*. This hit me on our first day in Iran. My tour guide asked me what I did for a living. How could I explain our show to a young man who'd never left Tehran? Do they have cartoons in Iran?

I began, "I write for this show called *The Simpsons* . . ."

"You know, I really liked the early seasons," he replied. "But even a bad *Simpsons* is better than a good *Family Guy*."

I thought about adopting him.

The Simpsons is the only thing Israelis and Egyptians agree on. In Iraq, fighting stopped from five to six every day so they could watch back-to-back episodes. If the show ran twenty-fours a day, we could bring peace to that land.

In Kurdistan, our guide Rebwar kept muttering, in a pretty good Julie Kavner impression, "Oh, I love my Homie."

In Singapore, I gave a speech and was mobbed by fans. Young women tore at my clothes and hair like I was Justin Bieber. It was horrifying, and I can't wait to go back.

I was in a restaurant in Malaysia when the waiter told me, "Homer Simpson is a very Malaysian father." Five minutes later, a Danish tourist said, "*The Simpsons* have a very Danish sense of humor." The Danish have a sense of humor?

Australians, Canadians, Indians, and Brits are crazy for the show. But nobody loves it like South Americans. They see the show dubbed into Spanish by a Mexican cast, and many of them believe *The Simpsons* is a show about a Mexican family. Our Mexican cast members used to earn only thirty dollars a week, except for Homer, who got forty dollars because he owns the microphone. (I'm not being racist—these are the facts!) Finally, our Mexican cast went on strike—not for more money, but for more dignity. And I thought, *You're the Mexican Homer Simpson! How much dignity do you expect?* (Okay, maybe now I'm being racist.)

In 1990, when the show was being translated for foreign markets, we did something most shows wouldn't go to the trouble of doing: we sent our writer, Jay Kogen, around the world, to supervise the voice casting. Jay did a remarkable job: the French voices for Marge and Homer fell in love and got married in 2001. If you ever wondered, *Would a woman like Marge ever marry a guy like Homer?* you only have to meet this couple. They're just like their characters: the wife is tall and prim, the husband squat and blunt. And like their characters, they seem crazy in love. *L'amour!*

People in every country tell me their *Simpsons* voices are better than ours—even the Czech Republic, where Marge is voiced by a man. And in Finland, I learned that children teach themselves to read just by watching *The Simpsons*—the show is in English there, with Finnish subtitles.

If you're wondering how these countries manage to translate our puns and wordplay, the answer is: They don't! All our clever sign jokes are left in English, with no translation. In Japan, when Bart called Moe's Tavern, saying, "I'd like to speak to Mr. Co-holic, first name Al," it was translated as, "I'm looking for a very drunken man." By my estimate, about one-third of our jokes are lost in translation. It doesn't matter—the two-thirds that foreigners get, they really, really like.

If you work in television, every time you see a TV—in a store, through someone's window—you hope they're watching your show. In Bolivia, that really happened: as wizened old Mayan women were weaving baskets, they watched our show on tiny black-and-white TVs. In fact, there were actually riots in Bolivia when they cut *Simpsons* reruns back from four a day to three. (EDITOR: Did this really happen? ME: Yes!) During my trip there, my Bolivian tour guide brought me to his home, a one-room flat with a family of five stuffed into two beds. They didn't have a kitchen. They didn't have a bathroom. But they had every piece of *Simpsons* merchandise I'd ever seen. *Simpsons* posters lined the walls; *Simpsons* glasses filled the cupboards. Matt Groening is rich because this guy is broke.

But our tour guide in Colombia may be the biggest *Simpsons* fan on earth. When he found out who I was, he bombarded me with *Simpsons* trivia questions for the next three days—apparently one joke that just didn't translate into Spanish was Homer's line about possums: "I call the big one Bitey."

Japan is the one big market *The Simpsons* can't crack. Apparently, the Japanese don't like the fact that the cartoon characters have four fingers—Disney actually goes to the expense of animating a fifth finger onto Mickey Mouse.

What bothers the Japanese about four fingers? You won't believe the reason: Yakuza members swear loyalty by amputating their pinkies, so having four fingers implies you're in the Japanese Mafia. Basically, the Japanese can't tell the Simpsons from the Sopranos. I spent weeks in Japan without seeing the show anywhere. I started to miss it. Finally, I told my tour guide I wrote for *The Simpsons*. His eyes lit up. "Really? That show is still on?"

"Yes, it is—thirty years!" I crowed.

"Wow—I can't believe I meet a man who writes *The Flintstones!*"

"Not *The Flintstones, The Simpsons*."

He looked puzzled. "You call it Simpstones?"

"No. Simpsons!"

"Flimpsons?"

I gave up. "Yes. I write the Flimpsons."

"Never heard of it."

While almost every country loved our show, the French hated it. Why? Because the French suck. Seriously, our first season we did an episode where Bart went to France . . . and the French pulled our show off the air for seventeen years. (The show has since returned, and the French now love it.)

This experience taught me something key about *The Simpsons*—Americans look at Homer Simpson and go, "That's my dad," while foreigners look at Homer Simpson and go, "That's an American." In fact, the nation of Venezuela canceled their run of the show because "it promotes bad American values." They pulled us off the air . . . and replaced us with *Baywatch*. (EDITOR: Did this really— ME: Yes, dammit!)

Nations who love the show suddenly don't find it funny when

the Simpson family visits their country. Famously, after the Simpsons went to Rio, the city's tourism board threatened to sue us. Their complaint read something like, "When the Simpsons came to Rio, they encountered pickpockets, kidnappers, rat-infested slums, and wild monkeys. There are no wild monkeys in Rio." I later visited Rio and saw hundreds of wild monkeys there. I also got robbed twice within four hours of arriving. The second robbery occurred forty feet from a cop who was sunning himself on the hood of his police car. He chose not to get involved. (EDITOR: Did— ME: YES, YES, AND YES!)

The weirdest reaction came after the Simpsons visited Canada. The next day, Canadians complained, "You didn't make enough fun of us, eh? There's a whole lot of dumb stuff here."

O Canada! Big country, small ego.

I've been asked to give my *Simpsons* lecture in twenty-one foreign countries, from Israel to India, China to Chile, Qatar to . . . well, nothing else starts with a Q.

In Qatar, I played to a packed house full of men in long white robes and women in burkas—people from every economic class, from millionaires to billionaires. These guys love *The Simpsons* and its irreverent wit, but they were shocked to hear it coming from an actual human being. (It's that weird paradox—when Homer strangles his son, it's funny; when you do it, it's a felony.) At one point I said, "I was asked not to show my *Queer Duck* cartoons today, because I was told there are no homosexuals in Qatar. Which is crazy, because I can see eight from where I'm standing."

There was a stunned silence followed by an explosion of laughter (which is the only kind of explosion you want to hear in the Middle East). One sheikh leaped from his seat and ran up and down the aisle—he couldn't contain his delight. They'd never seen anything like me—literally. The only other Jew in Qatar is in the Royal Zoo.

I've been to the North Pole . . .

. . . the South Pole . . .

. . . and wherever the hell this was.

Homer Simpson and Mr. Peabody

Every Christmas, the *Simpsons* producers give the staff a gift. Past examples include a skateboard with Bart's picture on it; a yellow bowling ball with Homer's name on it; a crystal ice bucket with Moe's face etched on it. (Moe's picture actually decreases its collectible value.) A lot of thought and a lot of time go into these presents—so much so that the staff Christmas gift sometimes comes in January. Or July. Or not at all. Still, these gifts are always appreciated by the writers and the cleaning ladies they regift them to.

In 2009, we all received a TomTom GPS that spoke in Homer's voice. This was a great gift, especially in those days before Waze and other phone apps. Dan Castellaneta spent four days in a studio recording Homer-ish directions: "Ooh, ooh, right turn ahead!" "Mmm . . . tunnel." Every journey ended with, "You have reached your destination and can hold your head up high because you are a genius."

It was very entertaining . . . for the first few trips. "After a while, those jokes get on your nerves," said Mike Price, and he's the *Simpsons* guy who wrote those jokes. Still, I stuck with the Homer GPS, unaware that I could change the voice setting to Blandly Soothing English Lady.

I put Homer to the test on one of our less exotic trips: Salem, Massachusetts. I set the GPS for the Peabody Essex Museum, and it brought me to a scruffy Revolution-era home. When I walked in, the tour guide seemed genuinely shocked to see a customer, saying, "Nobody ever comes here."

I told him, "My friend said the Peabody Essex is one of the great art museums of New England."

The guide said, "This isn't the Peabody Essex Museum, it's the George Peabody House Museum. You're not even in the right town!"

I felt like a fool, taking my driving directions from the stupidest man in cartoon history. Just then, the museum's phone rang, something else that rarely happened around there. The guide listened for a while and then turned to me. "It's the local paper—it's a slow news day and they're looking for a story. Are you anybody?"

"Kind of," I said. "I'm a writer for *The Simpsons*. In fact, I was directed here by a Homer Simpson GPS."

"Holy cow! What a story!" he exclaimed, as if I were the Lindbergh baby all grown up and had arrived with my wife, Amelia Earhart.

Minutes later, a car screeched up in front of the museum and a reporter raced in. This was the most excitement the George Peabody House Museum had seen since George Peabody died. The reporter breathlessly interviewed my wife and me, took our pictures, and roared away. Shortly after, I got directions—*written* directions and a map—to the *real* Peabody Essex Museum. It was as great as promised.

The next day, I was walking through downtown Peabody when a passing driver leaned out his window. "Hey, Homah Simpson!" he yelled in northeastern Massachusetts dialect. "You're a pissah."

Who is this guy? How does he know me? And why am I a pissah?

I spotted a newspaper box (remember those?) on the corner. Under a banner headline was the top story—the top story!—in the local paper: WORST GPS EVER GETS 'SIMPSONS' WRITER TO PEABODY. There was also a huge color photo of my wife and me. We would not merit a photo this huge if she had ridden me to victory in the Kentucky Derby. It really had been a slow news day.

When I got home, I gave the Homer Simpson GPS to my cleaning lady. She doesn't have a car or speak English, but she seemed to enjoy it.

The Worst Man in Australia

Australians love *The Simpsons,* except, naturally, the episode where the family goes there. That episode was condemned in the Australian parliament, which is a Hooters, by the way. They didn't object to us saying the Australian penal system involved kicking offenders with a giant boot, or that their prime minister's office was an inner tube in a pond. Nope. What they didn't like was our cast's attempt at doing an Australian accent. Mind you, the true Australian accent is semi-incomprehensible—and I use that term precisely. You can understand exactly one-half of what an Australian person says. Generally, it's the first half: "You know, if I was running your Congress I'd langa danga langa danga danga." But sometimes you can follow only the second half: "Langa danga langa danga and I woke up with a dead hooker covered in shrimp."

'I've made six wonderful trips Down Under and have met only one local who didn't love *The Simpsons*—he was my tour guide to the city of Cairns. What follows is a verbatim transcript from the long day we spent together:

TOUR GUIDE: So, what do you do for a living, mate?

ME: I write for a cartoon show called *The Simpsons*.

TOUR GUIDE: Well, that's a bloody stupid show.

ME: Gee, most people here seem to like it.

TOUR GUIDE: Oh, yeah, my daughter does. I can't tell you how many times I've had to smack her in the mouth for quoting your show.

ME: This is your daughter with leukemia?

TOUR GUIDE: That's the one. I can't abide the disrespect you people show to religion.

ME: That's funny, because the show was recently praised for its Christian values by Pope Benedict.

TOUR GUIDE: Well, he's a stupid wanker, i'n't he? [POINTING] Now, that over there is our new waterfront area. Bleedin' horrible. Developed by the Jews. They've got no sense of taste whatsoever.

ME: Um, you know I'm Jewish.

TOUR GUIDE (TAPS NOSE): Oh, I could tell, mate.

The tour came to an end with me wondering how much you tip an anti-Semitic child-beater. And that's when he said:

TOUR GUIDE: Here's my address. Do you think you could send my daughter an autographed script from your show?

ME: I'd be happy to.

TOUR GUIDE: And one for me, too?

FOUR PLACES TO DIE
BEFORE YOU SEE

I've been to more than a hundred countries, and had a great time in most of them. But here are a few you can skip:

1. **Ghana:** There are four long, skinny countries in West Africa, resembling four fingers. Three of them are very nice: Togo, Benin, and Côte d'Ivoire. The big fat middle finger is Ghana. This is the angriest place I've ever been—I saw a fistfight every day. One time, my driver jumped out of the cab and beat up a traffic cop. A big industry in Ghana is novelty coffins, hand-carved to look like pumpkins, pigeons, Porsches—you name it. It's a much better place to be dead than alive.

2. **Algeria:** French colonists left Algeria with two gifts—surliness and the baguette. Every morning, you see cranky Algerians walking around, noshing on yard-long loaves of French bread. They're cheap—the cost is subsidized by the government—so the locals eat as much as they want and drop the rest on the ground. By noon, the streets are ankle-deep with half-baguettes. It's a vaguely surreal sight—no wonder Camus set his novels here.

3. **Cuba:** Next time you see an article on "colorful, vibrant Cuba," look at the pictures. You can't get a decent photo of Havana because it's a crumbling, filthy city where nothing's been fixed since Meyer Lansky left. Castro did the impossible and turned a tropical paradise into a little slice of Cold War Hungary.

4. **Honduras:** The Springfield of nations. Visit a city
   known as "the most dangerous non-war zone on
   earth" and, even worse, "the birthplace of comedian
   Carlos Mencia." The national cuisine is Pizza Hut
   and Applebee's, and the service leaves something to
   be desired. Here's one verbatim exchange:

   WAITER: Tonight, our choices are chicken and fish.
   ME: Thanks. We'd like one of each.
   WAITER: And will you be joining us for dinner?
   ME: Yes. I'll have the chicken; my wife will have the
   fish.
   WAITER: Yes. And for the lady?
   ME: She'll have the fish.
   WAITER: Very good. Two fish.
   ME: Fine. Two fish.

   He brought our dinner two hours later: three beef
   burritos.
   In another restaurant, for reasons I never understood, I was literally—*literally*—chased out by an old
   lady with a butcher's knife. So much went wrong on
   my trip to Honduras that I often forget to mention I
   was kidnapped there—my tour driver threatened to
   dump me in the jungle unless I paid him a hundred
   dollars. When I refused, he lowered his demand
   to one hundred quetzals (twelve dollars). I still said
   no. Ultimately, the driver dumped us at our destination without stopping for our prepaid lunch. Yes, I
   was fifty-three years old and a bully stole my lunch
   money.

BURNING QUESTION

Why has the show lasted so long?

As I mentioned at the start of the book, before *The Simpsons* debuted, no one thought it would last more than six weeks. Back then, an offbeat show—even a great one, like *Police Squad!*—lasted an average of six weeks.

It's now been more than 1,500 weeks—going on thirty years—and *The Simpsons* is still in business. Thirty years—let this sink in. If the Simpsons had been aging like real people, Bart would be forty, Marge would be collecting Social Security, and Homer would have been dead for eight years.

What is the secret of the show's longevity? Critics and scholars have proposed theories that range from the wrong to the really, really, really wrong. No one's had a good explanation, and I finally realized we're all asking the wrong question. The question is "Why don't other shows last as long as *The Simpsons*?"

The answer is actors. Actors in live-action shows get bored doing the same role week after week. Jerry Seinfeld got tired of playing Jerry Seinfeld. The friends on *Friends* stopped being friends in real life. Only one live-action show lasted nearly as long as *The Simpsons,* and that's because it had a star who never complained. The show was called *Lassie.*

But animation goes on forever: *Family Guy* remains a hit after fifteen years; *South Park* is in its twenty-second season; and Mickey Mouse is still around after ninety years of creepy unfunniness.

Which raises the question: when will it end?

My response is always the same: Stop asking. It's rude. It's like saying, "Grandma, when are you going to die?" She doesn't know, and she doesn't want to think about it.

Even our producers grapple with this question. Every five years, they'll say, "Well, it's been twenty/twenty-five/thirty seasons—maybe we should wrap it up." This is like going to that same grandma and saying, "Nana, you're seventy-five—that's a nice round number. Drop dead."

None of the writers want the show to end. Not as long as we have stories to tell and ex-wives to support. Furthermore, no one is quite sure how to end the series. We've been pondering this for decades and nobody's had a good idea. Before the show ever came on the air, before we had any idea what it would become, Matt Groening had two ideas for a final episode:

1. Reveal that Krusty is really Homer. If you look at a design of Krusty without makeup, you'll see he looks just like Homer. Even though Bart loves Krusty and hates Homer, they're really the same guy!

2. Have Marge remove her tall bouffant hairdo to reveal long bunny ears beneath, like the long-eared rabbits in Matt's *Life in Hell* comic strip.

How's that for a series finale? Homer is Krusty and Marge is a giant rabbit. It's a wrap-up as irritating as the final *Seinfeld* and as baffling as the last *Lost*.

In 2011, the end of *The Simpsons* seemed a very real possibility. Our ratings were still high, but our budget was out of control: after two decades of incremental raises, even our janitor was pulling down $700,000 a year. Just when it looked like we needed a final episode, we got one: Stewart Burns wrote "Holidays of Future Passed." The show came back from Korean animation, and it was sweet, funny, and clever. A holiday show set thirty years from now, it revealed what the future held for all our characters. We had the perfect end to the series: *The Simpsons* began with a Christmas show; now it would end with one. Problem solved.

Then we got horrible news: we weren't canceled! Everyone at *The Simpsons*—the actors, the writers, even that janitor—took a pay cut. Why? Because we love our jobs and we love our show. "Holidays of Future Passed" aired seven years ago, so we still have no final show.

Maybe we'll just use our last episode to tie up loose ends: Maggie will finally talk; Grampa will drop dead; Mr. Burns will drop dead; Homer will shoot Flanders; Marge will shoot Homer. Then she'll take off her hair and reveal she's a rabbit.

ACT THREE

In a *Simpsons* script, act 3 is where we must wrap up the story . . . at which point we realize we don't have an ending. We try a lot of goofy stuff that gets rewritten more than any other part. In the end, running out of time and patience, we usually go with the last idea pitched, not the best one.

Act 3 of this book is sort of like that—my life after leaving *The Simpsons*: creating a memorable series (*The Critic*), an unmemorable series (*Teen Angel*), as well as children's books, animated films, and plays . . . all before realizing I was an idiot and running back to *The Simpsons*.

CHAPTER ELEVEN

ON COMEDY

Because this is a book about comedy, and because I'm being paid by the word, I thought I'd spend some time talking about comedy in general. Not that comedy can be taught: I've never taken a comedy writing class, nor have I worked with a comedy writer who has. Humor isn't something you study or analyze—it's just something you pick up. As a kid, you watch the shows that make you laugh and you begin to discriminate between the funny (Bugs Bunny) and the not funny (Woody Woodpecker). When I was six years old and watched Woody Allen do stand-up on *The Ed Sullivan Show,* I thought, *This guy really gets me.*

Comedy became my savior. As a kid, if you're bad at sports and not good-looking, you start trying to be funny yourself. You begin by repeating the great jokes you heard; then you try doing your own jokes in their style; finally, you do your own material. If no one laughs, you quit comedy and become a bitter alcoholic. But if they do laugh—ah, if they do!—you go into comedy and become a bitter alcoholic.

It's exactly the same as the way a baby learns to talk—the baby is just listening, trying to figure out what the hell is going on. Eventually the baby will babble a few sounds, and this will get amazing feedback from the parents. So the baby will learn a word, then a few more, and pretty soon the kid will be talking so much you wish he'd just shut the eff up. But no baby ever learns to talk from taking a class. You never meet a baby who says, "I'm studying talking with this professional talker down at the Learning Annex. Last week, he taught us 'ba-ba.'"

I was born three weeks early. My mom had gone to see the Jacques Tati comedy *Monsieur Hulot's Holiday,* and she laughed so hard she went into labor. I always thought this was an exciting origin story: "I am Comedy Man—born from the power of Laughter!" But twenty years later, I actually saw *Monsieur Hulot's Holiday,* and I couldn't figure out what my mom was laughing at. It's not that the jokes were bad; it's that they were nonexistent. Tati was a comedian only the French could love.

So why am I funny? (If you're thinking that I'm not funny, well, screw you!) I don't think I have a talent or a gift—I write comedy because I just can't help myself.

Exhibit A: I've traveled throughout the world, from Algeria to Zanzibar, and I've only gotten food poisoning once. It was from a health food restaurant in Beverly Hills. I lay in bed sweating and shivering for three days before I finally dragged myself to the emergency room. When the doctor asked me my symptoms, I told him in a string of jokes—this is how I talk: "Doc, my tongue is the color of Whoopi Goldberg, and I'm actually throwing up food other people ate. And stuff is oozing out of both ends of me—I'm like a human cannoli!"

The doctor laughed and called the nurses in: "Do it for them!"

So I did a second show for the nurses. I was dying . . . but I was killing.

The doctor patted me on the back. "Mr. Reiss, if you can make all these jokes, clearly you're not that sick." He sent me on my way.

An hour later, they found me collapsed in the hospital parking lot.

Exhibit B: My wife and I went to Hawaii on our honeymoon, and we visited Pearl Harbor. (This is a convenient symbol for how the whole honeymoon went.) We were standing over the wreck of the battleship *Arizona*—one of the most solemn spots in America—and I started laughing. Here's why: I looked over and saw a group of tourists from Tokyo, smiling and chatting away in Japanese. I imagined they were saying, "Nice work, boys. Look at the hole in that boat! This is a day that will live in famy."

Being funny is like being tall. People always ask me, "Are there ever days when you wake up and you're not funny?" No one asks Kobe Bryant, "Are there days when you wake up and you're not tall?"

Like Kobe Bryant, I'm just lucky there's a job that pays me to be this way. A century ago, someone like Kobe would work in a store—he'd be the guy you ask to get stuff off a high shelf; similarly, a guy like me would be locked in the basement of a madhouse, wrapped in cold, wet sheets.

But I'm not a madman, a genius, or an artist. I'm actually more like a chicken. Sometimes things form in my brain, and they get bigger and bigger, until I have to write them down just to free up some space in my head. It's the same way a chicken lays an egg. And when people eat that egg, the chicken is probably thinking, *Really? You like that? It just came out of my butt.*

I'm just lucky I can do this for a living, because I have no other skills. I can't sing or dance or play a musical instrument. I can't skate or ski or speak a foreign language. I typed this whole book with one finger.

So what would I do if I couldn't write comedy? I'd write for Jimmy Fallon. Look at it: "Fallon" is kind of just "no laff spelled backward.

The fact is, if I couldn't write comedy, I'd probably be a funny lawyer. The kind who gets a lot of laughs in court. And then his client goes to the electric chair. For shoplifting. (I told that joke in Qatar, and a Saudi Arabian in the audience went, "Yeah? So?")

There were three great comedians in my formative years—Bill Cosby, Bill Murray, and Richard Pryor—and they wrecked comedy for a generation. How? By never saying anything funny. You can quote a Steve Martin joke, or a Rodney Dangerfield line, but Pryor, Cosby, and Murray? The things they said were funny only when *they* said them. In Cosby's case, it didn't even need to be sentences: "The thing of the thing puts the milk in the toast, and ha, ha, ha!" It was gibberish and America loved it.

The problem was that they inspired a generation of comedians who tried coasting on personality—they were all attitude and no jokes. It was also a time when comedy stars didn't seem to care. Bill Murray made some lousy movies; Richard Pryor and Eddie Murphy made even more; and any script that was too lame for these guys, Chevy Chase made. These were smart people—they had to know how bad these films were, but they just grabbed a paycheck and did them. Most of these comic actors started as writers—they could have written their own scripts, but they rarely bothered.

Then, at the end of a decade of lazy comedy and half-baked material, *The Simpsons* came along. We cared about jokes, and we worked endless hours to cram as many into a show as possible. I'm not sure we can take all the credit, but TV and movies started trying harder. Jokes were back. Shows like *30 Rock* and *Arrested Development* demanded that you pay attention. These days, comedy stars like Seth Rogen, Amy Schumer, Kristen Wiig, Melissa McCarthy, and Jonah Hill actually write the comedies they star in.

So what is comedy? I've spent my whole life making it, and yet

I have no idea. I've read all the philosophers on humor—Aristotle, Freud, Henri Bergson—and they're completely clueless. The latest theory, according to a fascinating book called *The Humor Code*, calls comedy an act of "benign transgression." For example:

Why did the chicken cross the road?
It was an act of benign transgression.

I think all these theories are nonsense. Comedy is too weird and wonderful and subjective to have an overarching theory. I mean, what unites Nichols and May with Cheech and Chong? Nothing, except that they both suck.

I do have a theory of jokes, however. It's not comprehensive or profound, but it's an observation I've never heard anyone else make: When a joke is over, it's over. All the loose ends are tied up, the journey is complete. All the weirdness that preceded the punchline now makes sense. Here's an example:

A duck walks into a pharmacy and asks for ChapStick. The druggist says, "Will that be cash or credit?" And the duck says, "You can put it on my bill."

Think of all the questions this story raises: Why is a duck in a pharmacy? Why does he need ChapStick? He has no lips. He can talk, too? But none of this surprises the druggist; he's just worried how he's going to get paid.

But with that punchline—"You can put it on my bill"—all those questions collapse. In a crazy twist of logic, it all starts to make sense: we have no further questions, and we don't care whether the duck gets over his case of chapped bill. The hell with him.

I love the illogical logic of some jokes. Take this line by George Carlin: "Beethoven was so deaf he thought he was a painter." It kind of makes sense.

(I consider Carlin the greatest comedian ever. He delivered his jokes beautifully, and they're funny even when I steal them.)

A joke doesn't have to be illogical, either—sometimes a punchline wraps it up like a tidy mystery story. Let me close by telling one of my favorites:

A bartender is closing up shop and sees a patron lying on the floor. He picks him up, the guy falls down. He picks him up, the guy falls down. Finally, the bartender slings the guy over his shoulder and carries him to an address he finds in the guy's wallet. When they get to the guy's house, the bartender stands him up again—he crumples in a heap.

The bartender bangs on the door and the guy's wife answers. "Here's your drunken bum of a husband," the bartender says.

The wife asks, "Where's his wheelchair?"

Great Comedies You've Never Seen (But Should!)

The American Film Institute made a list of the hundred greatest comedies of all time, called "AFI: 100 Years . . . 100 Laughs." That works out to one laugh per year, or roughly what Dane Cook has given me.

The AFI list is very solid, with lots of movies you really should see: *Annie Hall, Animal House, Airplane!, Groundhog Day* . . . all the usual suspects. I don't really care for their top two picks: *Tootsie* (a man in a dress?) and *Some Like It Hot* (two men in dresses?), although I do like number sixty-seven, *Mrs. Doubtfire* (a man in an old-lady dress).

Nazis don't seem funny, but they score three films on the list, the Hitler hat trick: *The Producers, To Be or Not to Be,* and *The Great Dictator.* But where are the funny zombies? There's a surprising number of great zombie comedies and none of them made the list: *Zombieland, Shaun of the Dead, Dead Alive, Evil Dead II, Army of Darkness,* and the deeply satirical *Dawn of the Dead,* where zombies stumble around a mall like brain-dead consumers.

You should see every one of Tex Avery's hilarious cartoons, as well as the live-action cartoons they inspired: *The Mask, Kung Fu Hustle,* and *Who Framed Roger Rabbit.* The Marx Brothers have four films on the AFI list, but they made a couple of later films that are very underrated: *Go West* and *A Night in Casablanca.*

And any comedy fan has to see the documentary *The Aristocrats.* In it, seventy-five different comedians tell the exact same joke—and it's not even a very good joke. But they all tell it in different styles, and it demonstrates how many different ways there are to be funny. It's also the Olympics of comedy, as you judge which comic tells the joke the best. I agree with the filmmakers' choice: Gilbert Gottfried.

Finally, here's a list of great comedies you've never seen and probably never heard of:

1. *One, Two, Three* (1961): Billy Wilder mixes the Cold War with the cola wars in this film about a Coke executive in West Berlin. The movie revs up to a breakneck comic clip for its whole second hour. The pace was so grueling, star Jimmy Cagney quit acting for the next twenty years.

2. *Top Secret!* (1984): The makers of *Airplane!* followed that hit with this fizzle. The movie's not ha-ha funny, but it's definitely weird funny, filled with great surreal jokes, like the Nazi falling off a tower and shattering like glass on the ground. If you were disappointed in its original release, give it another look.

3. *Hot Fuzz* (2007): Simon Pegg writes great films for himself, and his small-town cop flick has one of the

best-constructed screenplays ever. There's not one line in the film's first half that doesn't pay off in the second.

4. *The High Sign* (1921): The first film directed by Buster Keaton, and the only movie I've ever considered to be *too* funny. It's so stuffed with inspired comedy, I wish it had been spread out over two or three films.

5. *The Man with Two Brains* (1983): One of Steve Martin's funniest films and one of his biggest duds. It's just pure jokes, most of them great.

6. *Ni Vu, Ni Connu* (1958): This French tale of a poacher and a cop is the funniest film you never, ever heard of. I stumbled on it at the Museum of Modern Art; I have no idea where you can see it. I can't even translate the title!

The Six Greatest Books About Comedy (Besides the One You're Holding)

1. *Born Standing Up: A Comic's Life:* Steve Martin takes you through the many years it took him to develop his comedy persona. It's a very serious book about being funny.

2. *Wake Me When It's Funny:* Garry Marshall has dozens of hilarious stories about breaking into TV comedy and eventually conquering the medium.

3. *Even This I Get to Experience:* Norman Lear doing the same thing as Garry Marshall (above). These first three are even better as audiobooks, read with comic panache by their authors.

4. *Sick in the Head: Conversations About Life and Comedy:* Judd Apatow interviews pretty much every comedian alive in the quickest 576 pages you'll ever breeze through.

5. *American Cornball: A Laffopedic Guide to the Formerly Funny:* The only scholarly analysis on humor that gets it right. Author Christopher Miller catalogs hundreds of great comic clichés that have faded into the past, like absentminded professors, naked guys wearing barrels, and safes falling on people's heads. He explains that the Simpsons family therapy scene where they electrocute each other is "just a pie fight with electricity." I wrote that scene and never realized it, but he's right!

6. *Poking a Dead Frog: Conversations with Today's Top Comedy Writers:* Don't pay for a comedy writing class; everything you need to know is in this book by Mike Sacks. Comedy writers in every field of entertainment describe how they create humor and offer solid, practical advice on getting a job.

Tweets for the Sweet

I loved everything about the abovementioned *Poking a Dead Frog* except the title: what the hell does that mean? The book even taught me something new: that late-night comedy shows are recruiting their writers from Twitter. It's a great showcase for young writers—*The Simpsons'* newest staff member, Megan Amram, got her start on Twitter, amassing 700,000 followers. It's also a great training tool for aspiring writers—the 280-character limit enforces brevity, a comic necessity, and the number of likes and retweets provides instant feedback on how funny the jokes is.

And so, at the age of fifty-seven, I started tweeting, and even after thirty-five years as a professional, it's making me a better comedy writer. Follow me at @MikeReissWriter. Here's a sampling:

OJ leaves prison: I just want to be left alone so I can shiv a former wife. Whoops! I mean 'live a normal life.'

- - - - - - - - - - -

Chevy Chase turns 74 today. Thanks for all the year of laughter and all the great movie.

- - - - - - - - - - -

To those who say name is destiny, I counter with Pete Best, Donny Most, and Cedric the Entertainer.

- - - - - - - - - - -

Justin Timberlake sees a doctor:

JT: Got this feeling in my body

DR: I really need more to go on.

JT: I can't stop the feeling

DR: It's MS.

- - - - - - - - - - -

NEWS: MAN BURNS AT "BURNING MAN"
His last words: "The irony stings. But what really hurts is the burning."

- - - - - - - - - - -

Trump doesn't act like a President. He acts like Gary Busey playing a President.

- - - - - - - - - - -

Jimi Hendrix would be seventy-five this month. If he'd lived, he'd be dead by now.

- - - - - - - - - - -

"The cabin boy, the pastry chef
The Gustaffson Fam-i-ly

Dave Pendergast and the rest . . ."
—The 9 people who died in the wreck of the SS Minnow

⸺

If you're looking for good news in these turbulent times, think of this: Julia Roberts hardly ever makes movies anymore.

⸺

Hidden message in my note to Trump: first letter of lines!
You suck
Oh, you suck
U suck
Suck, you do
U suck
Christ, you suck
Know what? You suck

⸺

Unlike Coldplay songs, no two snowflakes are exactly the same.

⸺

After a long battle with depression, Charlie Brown has killed himself. Friends, family overcome with good grief.

⸺

Wouldn't it be cool if George Romero died and came back as a zombie?
Or George Lucas died and came back as a robot?
Or Michael Bay died?

⸺

"Madman Lures Five Children to Abandoned Building—Four Die."
    —Synopsis of Willie Wonka & the Chocolate Factory

CHAPTER TWELVE

HOW KRUSTY BECAME *THE CRITIC*

As Al and I were completing our two years running *The Simpsons,* Matt Groening came to us with a new idea: an animated Krusty the Clown spin-off. We developed the concept, imagining Krusty as a single dad in New York, with a crabby makeup lady and a crazy, Ted Turner–like boss.

Matt turned us down, deciding he'd rather do a live-action Krusty "reality show" in which Dan Castellaneta (who voices the character) would go around having adventures, like working on a tuna boat or delivering a baby.

That makes two shows that didn't happen.

A year later, in 1993, Jim Brooks told us he wanted to do a sitcom set at a morning program like the *Today* show. Al and I kicked it around, and decided to focus on the show's Gene Shalit–like movie critic. We fleshed it out with all the rejected Krusty show ideas: single dad in New York, crabby makeup lady, Ted Turner boss. Comedy, like composting, involves smart recycling.

Jim liked the idea and asked us if we were fans of Jon Lovitz— he'd just seen him in Penny Marshall's *A League of Their Own.*

We loved Lovitz and had had him on *The Simpsons* three times. Al and I were more than happy to develop a live-action "critic pilot" for Lovitz. But we neglected to tell Lovitz. When we finally presented a finished script to him, he said, "I can't do a TV show! I'm a MOVIE STAR!!!" (Said in the most Lovitz way possible.)

In all fairness, he did have three movies lined up: *City Slickers II: The Legend of Curly's Gold, Trapped in Paradise,* and Rob Reiner's *North.* (Lovitz would later say, "Three movies, thrrree BOMBS!")

Lovitz was about to walk out of our meeting when Al and I said, in desperation, "What if it's animated?"

Just like that, he was in, and *The Critic* was born. It became the only animated show in history where the very last creative decision was to make it a cartoon.

Based on the success of *The Simpsons,* Jim Brooks got a great deal with ABC. No matter what idea he came in with, they had to make twenty-two episodes of it. They couldn't say no.

Excitedly, we went with Jim to ABC with the pitch: an animated show about a film critic, starring Jon Lovitz.

"No," they said.

After some negotiation, they finally agreed to make thirteen episodes. This was the start of *The Critic*'s rocky road on TV.

Ya Gotta Lovitz

I first saw Jon Lovitz when I was working at *The Tonight Show.* L.A.'s improv troupe the Groundlings were guests, and a very young Lovitz performed his character Tommy Flanagan, the pathological liar. Even then, I saw he was special.

I met Jon years later at a *Simpsons* table reading where he was guest-starring as Marge's prom date Artie Ziff. Before we began, I mentioned a story from the newspaper: "It says thieves are cutting off people's hands in downtown L.A. to get their Rolexes."

"You mean like THIS ONE?" said Jon, shoving his fat Rolex in my face. He is the master of upbeat bluster and unearned self-confidence. But is that the real Jon Lovitz?

It's an interesting philosophical point: it's not who Jon is; it's merely a character he plays twenty-four hours a day. In unguarded moments, Jon can be shy and self-critical. He's always apologizing to me for no good reason.

JON LOVITZ APOLOGIZES FOR NO GOOD REASON

"I would get all frustrated, and sometimes I'd give Mike and Al a hard time. I felt bad about that, because they couldn't have been nicer. I actually apologized to Mike about giving him a hard time, and he said, 'I don't have any memory of that. I just always remember your being very nice and very pleasant.' *Oh good!* Because sometimes I do get a little cranky."

Jon also plays classical piano, speaks fluent French, and sings opera. His stage debut was in—picture this—*Death of a Salesman*.

On *The Critic* we surrounded him with a truly eclectic cast, ranging from the voice of Babe, the sheepherding pig (Christine Kavanaugh), to soft-core porn actor Charles Napier. We had the world's greatest impressionist (Maurice LaMarche) and the man of a thousand accents (Nick Jameson); between them, they'd do sixty characters per episode—and we paid by the character! Everyone's favorite actor on the show wasn't an actor at all—the role of the makeup woman, Doris, was played by Doris Grau, *The Simpsons'* script supervisor.

The hardest part to cast was Margo, critic Jay Sherman's sympathetic sister. We hired and fired four different actresses, including Margaret Cho, before realizing the perfect Margo was right in front of us: Nancy Cartwright.

"For me," Nancy said, "it was fantastic because I wasn't Bart, Nelson, Ralph, Kearney, Database, Todd Flanders . . . I was actually going to get to play a *girl*! I had some ideas at first, but then they just said they wanted me to do it as *me*."

Designing these characters was a lot harder. We didn't have a visionary artist like Matt Groening, so we put together an amazing team: David Silverman (*The Simpsons*), Rich Moore (*Wreck-It Ralph*), Everett Peck (*Duckman*), and David Cutler (*The Nightmare Before Christmas*). I'm afraid we designed it by committee, with us nonartistic producers mixing and matching different parts of different characters. It was a Frankenstein process, and some people said Jay Sherman even looked like Frankenstein, with his flat square head. Once the show debuted, we learned that Jay was coincidentally a dead ringer for real-life film critic James Wolcott.

PHOTO UNAVAILABLE

It turns out Jay Sherman looked just like *Vanity Fair* critic James Wolcott. You'll have to Google him to find out—it also turns out it's easier to print a picture of Muhammad than James Wolcott.

Al and I gave Jay Sherman two memorable catchphrases: "It stinks!" (which needs no explanation) and "Hotchie-motchie!" (which needs lots). I heard "Hotchie-motchie!" just once as a kid, and I never forgot it. It was a cry of dismay uttered by a member of Hermine's Royal Lilliputians, a troupe of performing little people.

We hired a crackerjack writing team, about half of them Harvard film nerds—in fact, *The Critic*'s Slavic restaurateur, Vlada, was named after our film professor Vlada Petric. (The character design of Vlada is based on Hungarian *Simpsons* animator Gábor Csupó.)

It was a boys' club—about a dozen men working on the whole production. But in our defense, two of those twelve men have since become women. Top that, *Transparent*!

We also had a consulting writer on the show—a funny kid who'd come in one or two days a week. His name was Judd Apatow.

JUDD APATOW ON WORKING AT *THE CRITIC*

"Mike and Al had an enormous amount of energy and patience. They did something I've never seen anybody do since: *They didn't get up all day long.* We would go in and it would be like ten in the morning until sometimes between eight and ten at night. And Mike and Al wouldn't stand up all day! They would just sit in their chairs. Al would have a cup filled with M&M's and peanuts and pretzels and whatever he was grazing on. And they would just pitch jokes for ten to twelve straight hours. They almost never even left the room to listen to sound mixes or have meetings. Now that I've run shows, I've always wondered, *When did they have* meetings? I don't remember Mike and Al ever leaving the room! They just had such patience and loved being in the room."

A Tale of Two Critics

The Critic debuted to great ratings and rave reviews. Two days later, my assistant Dee walked in with a large cardboard box, bulging at the seams.

"What's that?" I asked.

"Hate mail," she replied.

The sensibility that had served us so well on *The Simpsons* was too raw and edgy for ABC's family-friendly audience. Viewers were particularly incensed by a scene where Jay sleeps with an actress on their first date. (I'm glad we cut the line where the critic says, "Even my orgasms feel better!") Ironically, throughout our run, we were the top-rated show on TV among children—even bigger than *The Simpsons*.

The ratings eroded fast, and ABC pulled us off the air after six weeks. Despite this annoyance, they had been very supportive throughout the entire process. At a meeting with network president Bob Iger, he gestured to a wall-size chart of ABC's programs and asked, "Where on this schedule do you see your show fitting in?"

I muttered, "Sunday night, on Fox, after *The Simpsons*."

And that's just where we went.

Jim Brooks managed to move *The Critic* from ABC to Fox. It was a huge deal, requiring the cooperation of French and German production companies. It was the first time those two countries had collaborated since the Vichy government. It turned out to be just as successful.

Fox slated us to go on after *The Simpsons*—they'd tried eight different series in that slot, and nothing had worked. To launch the series, Jim Brooks decided we'd do a crossover episode on *The Simpsons,* where the critic judges the Springfield Film Festival.

Crossovers are a television tradition: *The Beverly Hillbillies* visited *Petticoat Junction; The Love Boat* went to *Fantasy Island;* the Jetsons crossed time to meet the Flintstones. Jim Brooks did them all the time, mixing characters from his three sitcoms, *The Mary Tyler Moore Show, Rhoda,* and *Phyllis.* As a kid, I used to love crossovers—they showed me that all these characters on different shows lived in the same universe and that they were all friends.

When it came time to do the episode, there was a huge outcry from the *Simpsons* staff. Showrunner David Mirkin was on board with it, but the rest of the staff said, "*WE WILL NOT ALLOW THIS!*"

What was especially hurtful was that our most vocal opponents were also our friends. People Al and I had hired onto *The Simpsons* were fighting against us.

But the loudest mouth in the room belonged to a writer who had just been hired at the show. He'd been there only a few weeks, but decided he knew best what was appropriate for *The Simpsons.* (He didn't last long at the show.)

We went to Jim Brooks to report on the insurrection, and he uttered one of my favorite lines in a lifetime of great lines: "When did this become a democracy?"

We proceeded to do the episode, entirely written and produced by the *Critic* staff.

The *Simpsons* writers had put up so much resistance that we worked extra hard to make it a great show. It has since become a fan favorite, generating at least one classic *Simpsons* line: While everyone at the film festival is booing Mr. Burns, he asks Smithers, "Are they saying boo?"

Smithers replies, "No, they're saying *boo-urns! Boo-urns!*"

When the show finally aired, all the *Simpsons* writers who'd opposed the idea were contractually still able to get producing credit on the episode if they wanted it. Indeed they wanted it; they all took a paycheck for it, too. Every one of them took credit and pay for a show where their only contribution was trying to keep it from happening.

Well, not everyone. The one person who *didn't* take credit was

Matt Groening, who discreetly took his name off the show. I don't think we noticed at first, and I believe it's the only time on any *Simpsons* episode that Matt's name doesn't appear in the credits. This led someone in postproduction to leak the fact to the *Los Angeles Times,* which ran with the story. Matt said he did it because it "violates the *Simpsons* universe," adding, "Through all the years of *The Simpsons,* we have been careful about maintaining their uniqueness."

Jim Brooks came to our defense, saying Matt was ungrateful for all the work we had done on his show: "For years, Al and Mike were two guys who worked their hearts out on this show, staying up until four in the morning to get it right. . . . *The Critic* is their shot and he should be giving them his support."

This was Antietam at *The Simpsons,* the bloodiest conflict of our Civil War, and in hindsight, it wasn't that big a deal.

Still, there was so much bitterness over it that years later, when we were doing DVD commentary on the episode, all that resentment came pouring out. It was so bilious that Jim said, "This is terrible—we can't use this." So, for the only time in our history, we erased the track and did a second commentary. Jim gets mad on that one, too!

Matt Groening and I have laughed about it since. *The Simpsons* would go on to do crossovers with *Family Guy, The X-Files,* and *Futurama.* Matt had no problem with that last one.

He Who Must Not Be Named

The president of Fox who bought *The Critic* to put on after *The Simpsons* got fired before the show actually aired. The new president who came in just hated the show.

The Critic got stellar ratings in its debut on Fox. He called, not to congratulate us, but to say, "How well do you think it will do without any publicity?" *Huh?* We had just given him a successful show and here he was refusing to publicize it.

We were all baffled. Lovitz recalls, "I called Jim Brooks to see why it was happening, and he said, 'I've never seen anything like this.'"

We aired ten episodes on Fox, and the network president phoned after eight of them to say how much he hated the show.

Once he called us in for a meeting. He played an episode on his monitor to demonstrate how "bad" our show was. When his staff started laughing, he snapped at them, "Why are you laughing? This isn't funny!"

After six weeks, he canceled the show and replaced it with a series he had developed called *House of Buggin'*. Maybe the problem with *The Critic* was not enough buggin'.

The final irony was that this guy quit as Fox president a few months later. He came, canceled our show, and left without a trace. It was like he was a demon from hell summoned up solely to cancel *The Critic* before descending back into the fiery cauldron where he belongs.

There's a rule in show business that you never badmouth anyone by name, because somewhere down the road, you may want to work with them again. That's usually a good rule.

But this Fox president was named John Matoian.

John Matoian. John Matoian. John Matoian. John Matoian. John Matoian.

The next year we had an offer to revive *The Critic* at UPN, a new network that had just started up. But they wanted to dumb down our content and shift the focus from Jay Sherman to his son, Marty, and his child friends. I said no, that wasn't the show. Plus, I couldn't bear the possibility of being canceled on three networks in three years.

The Critic was not dead yet. During the 2000 dot-com boom, Al and I were asked to make original *Critic* shorts for the internet. We'd be using Flash animation, meaning we could produce a cartoon in nine days instead of nine months. We'd be able to parody movies while they were still in theaters. Al and I reunited the old cast and wrote and produced ten short cartoons. Then, for reasons I'll never understand, the production company sat on the shorts for ten months. It actually took longer to get shorts on the net than to do fully animated episodes for the networks.

That production company went bust, and *The Critic* was finally finished. It was fun making the show and I loved working with Lovitz. But in two years with the guy, he never learned my name. He always referred to Al Jean and me as "Al and Jean." That's one thing he could apologize for . . .

More than two decades later, people still tell me how much they

Lovitz respects me as his boss.

love the series. It's hard to believe about a show full of parodies of now-obscure nineties movies. It's a little dated—in fact, every single episode opens with a shot of the World Trade Center!

You can still see *The Critic* on the Crackle and Reelz networks, and crisp copies of every episode are posted on YouTube. We're still considering partnering with the Jehovah's Witnesses to go door-to-door with the show. Because it's our belief that there's no medium so small *The Critic* can't fail in it.

I'll give the last word to Jon Lovitz, the guy who didn't want to do the show in the first place (because he's a MOVIE STAR!):

"If you go on my Twitter feed, every week you can see people asking about it. And I'd love to do it again. I've tried. But Al's doing *The Simpsons,* and Mike said go ahead but he doesn't want to do it himself. I'd do a Kickstarter, I'd do this or that. I even said, 'Why don't we do it as a live sitcom? But it's just sitting there . . . and meanwhile millions of fans want it back."

AL JEAN ON *THE CRITIC*

"I think the last thing Mike and I argued about was a thing in *The Critic*. We were doing a parody of Orson Welles doing a commercial about peas. I think I wanted to extend it into the black or something, and he didn't. That would have been twenty-two years ago. The last creative difference we had."

(AUTHOR'S NOTE: Al wanted Orson Welles to say, after exiting screen, "Oh, what luck! There's a French fry stuck in my beard," followed by eating noises. It seemed like overkill. I hated the joke . . . and every single other person on planet Earth loved it. LOVED IT! Someone recently posted the clip on Twitter, calling it "one of the greatest jokes in TV history." I guess Al was right.)

BURNING QUESTION

What's the biggest reason *The Critic* failed?

Al and I were the first *Simpsons* alumni to create our own animated series. We didn't want to encroach on their territory, so we decided to make *The Critic* as different from *The Simpsons* as possible:

They were suburban; we were urban.

They featured a married couple; we had a divorced dad.

They were middle-class; we were wealthy.

Homer was dumb; Jay Sherman was too smart for his own good.

All this deliberate distancing resulted in another difference: they were a hit; we were a dud.

Nowadays, television is much more experimental, audiences

more fractured, and people more in need of novelty. But back in the nineties, the way you created a hit show was to take an existing hit and change one thing about it:

Seinfeld's a hit? Give him a wife, you've got *Mad About You*. Throw in some kids—it's *Everybody Loves Raymond*. Make it suck—and it's *Home Improvement*.

But there's an even more fundamental reason *The Critic* failed, and it's so obvious, no one's ever noticed: Every animated series that's succeeded on the big four networks has been about a family. Every single one: *The Flintstones*, *The Jetsons*, *The Simpsons*, *King of the Hill*, *Family Guy*, *American Dad*, *Bob's Burgers*.

This doesn't just hold for animation, either. For decades, TV's top-rated sitcom was about a family. The torch would be passed from show to show: *The Beverly Hillbillies* to *All in the Family* to *The Cosby Show* to *Roseanne*. People, it seems, would rather watch a family than spend time with their own.

It even helps to have "family" in the title: *Family Ties*, *Family Affair*, *Family Guy*, *Family Matters*. Mike Nichols even produced a series that was just called *Family*.

But that last one was a flop. I trust the stupid copyeditor will remember to take that out.

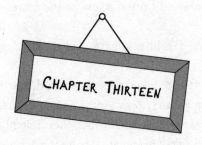

Chapter Thirteen

A DEVELOPMENT DEAL WITH
THE DEVIL

After the failure, resurrection, and refailure of *The Critic,* Al Jean and I decided to cash in on our lack of success. We got a development deal.

Development deals were a phenomenon where a studio would pay you a lot of money to create TV shows for them exclusively. The studios would then sell the shows to networks; the shows would fail, as 95 percent of shows do, and everyone would lose money.

Eventually the studios realized that they'd save money by *not* making TV shows, so they would shoot down virtually any idea pitched to them. Years later, they finally figured out that they'd save even more money by not making development deals at all. The whole business model faded away, a quaint relic of the 1990s like Hulk Hogan or unbiased news.

Al and I met with several studios about making a deal. At DreamWorks, Steven Spielberg himself sat down with us. He said, "I love *The Critic,* but you held Jon back. Let Lovitz be Lovitz."

I quipped, "Steve, I think I know a little more about directing than you do."

The joke played to utter silence, and we didn't get the Dream-Works deal.

Al and I made a three-year development deal with another studio. Over the next thirty-six months, we pitched them more than a hundred series ideas, none of which they bought. One we really liked was called *Forty Below*: it was about a team of research scientists stuck at a base at the South Pole. Ten years before *The Big Bang Theory* and sixteen years before *Frozen,* we had a sitcom that combined them both. And drawing off what we learned at *The Simpsons,* we did our homework, reading every book we could find about Antarctica.

When we finished our pitch, the studio executive had one suggestion: "Set it at the North Pole."

I told him we couldn't and he asked, "What's the difference?"

"It's literally all the difference in the world," I explained. "There's land at the South Pole. The North Pole is all ice and water. You can't build a base there!"

He let this sink in, then said, "I still think it should be the North Pole."

"WHY?" I asked, exasperated.

"It's a funnier pole."

Forty Below never went anywhere.

Al and I continued to do good work during this time. Just not on our development deal. We were moonlighting at *The Simpsons,* producing episodes on the side with a separate crew of writers. We did some pretty good shows, including "Simpson Tide" (Homer and Bart on a navy sub), "*Simpsoncalifragilisticexpiala(Annoyed Grunt)cious*" (our *Mary Poppins* parody), and "The Springfield Files," our crossover with *The X-Files.* This last idea had been gathering dust at *The Simpsons* for four years, the longest development of any episode in history.

Back at the studio, after two and a half years of rejection, we decided to take the hack writer approach: we combined two successful shows to form a third one. We went to ABC with the idea for *Teen Angel:* "It's a cross between *Beavis and Butt-Head* and *Sabrina, the Teenage Witch.*"

"We love it," said the ABC executives, pleased that we were finally getting it. "But we don't like the *Beavis and Butt-Head* angle."

"So you want it to be a cross between *Sabrina*?" I asked.

They nodded. And that's what we gave them: the story of a teenage boy whose best friend dies and comes back as a mischievous guardian angel. It was like *The Odd Couple* but with a funny new twist: teen death. We found wonderful actors for the two teens, but for the role of the mother, ABC insisted we cast Maureen McCormick: Marcia Brady. Maureen is a lovely lady and a good actress, but she just looked too young: she was playing the mother of a teenager—and she still looked like a teenager! It gave the show a creepy hillbilly-incest vibe. But ABC insisted we hire her. Twelve episodes later, ABC insisted we fire her. Five episodes after that, they canceled the show.

We had a talented team of writers who would go on to do much better shows like *Frasier* and *The Big Bang Theory*. But *Teen Angel* had this feeling of crushing gravity—it was an ABC show on TGIF (This Garbage Is Feeble) and as hard as we worked, we couldn't escape Planet Mediocrity. My name sometimes appeared three times on an episode—as creator, writer, and producer—and even I couldn't stand the show.

The fans have been kinder to *Teen Angel*—the show scores a 7.4 on IMDb. That puts it in a tie with *The Critic* and just a skosh below *Cheers* (7.8).

I had one other job during my dismal development deal. I was a consulting writer on *Homeboys in Outer Space,* a sci-fi parody about bumbling interstellar deliverymen. It was a cross between *Futurama* and . . . well, it was really just *Futurama,* three years before *Futurama*. (Pure coincidence—no one would knowingly rip off *Homeboys*.)

The show's creator, Ehrich Van Lowe, assembled an amazing staff of newcomers. Four of them would become founding writers on *Family Guy* and later create *American Dad*. Actor Kevin Michael Richardson and writer Mike Price went from *Homeboys* to *The Simpsons*. When *Homeboys in Outer Space* premiered, the *Los Angeles Times* called it "the best new comedy of the season."

And then the executives got involved: they shot down every story pitched to them and assigned us a supervisor who told us, "I come from soap operas. I don't get comedy." This once-promising show was canceled after twenty-one episodes and would wind up on *TV Guide*'s list of "Fifty Worst Shows of All Time."

To recap: studio executives turned "the best new comedy" into "the worst of all time" in under one year. Thank you for your service.

Al Jean put it best: "A development deal is where a studio pays you a lot of money for the privilege of ruining your career."

I Quit!

Following our development debacle, Al Jean and I amicably ended our seventeen-year partnership. He went right back to *The Simpsons*—I quit show business, vowing never to return. I'd seen the development process close up and believed nothing of quality could ever come out of it. For fifteen years, I'd followed the classic career trajectory—staff writer, producer, showrunner, development deal, and finally series creator—and found it got less and less fun at every step.

I thought I'd never write again. I traveled the world with my wife, went to museums and movies, and just enjoyed myself. I had enough money saved to last me the rest of my life, unless I wanted to eat or live indoors.

And yet, I couldn't stop writing. It wasn't for money or prestige or career advancement—it was just something I did. I wrote whatever I felt like: children's books, *New Yorker* pieces, short stories, editorials.

And every bit of it got rejected. I amassed 150 rejection letters in my first year of semiretirement.

I thought about giving up—wouldn't you? And then I read about Jack London, the bestselling, most translated author of his time. Before he got published, he racked up a pile of rejection letters on a spindle three feet tall.

And then slowly, I started getting acceptances. All my *New Yorker* rejects were published in *Esquire*. One of these pieces wound up in a textbook on how to write humor. Screw you, Shouts & Murmurs.

My book *How Murray Saved Christmas* was read and rejected by a dozen children's book publishers. But then I found my lucky thirteenth. They published the book everyone else had read and rejected. It was a massive hit. In a business where 9,000 sales makes a bestseller, this book sold 160,000 copies. It later became an animated holiday special.

Since then, I've continued to write projects that I've truly believed in. I've sold eighteen children's books and eight movie scripts, and punched up two dozen animated films. It's all been fun, and I'm earning just what I used to make on the Hollywood treadmill.

My lesson to young comedy writers is to avoid the traditional path and do the work you love. Or don't. This may work out horribly for you.

Anyway, writing for TV was a huge part of my career, but it was only half my life. What follows is the second half.

The boring half.

AL JEAN ON MY RETIREMENT

"When Mike said he was retiring, what he was retiring *from* was running a show day to day. I think that bothered him a lot. When we were on *Teen Angel,* we would literally have like a dozen people giving us notes on episodes. Contradictory notes, notes that contradicted what the person himself said a week earlier. I think that's what set him off: he just got more tired of dealing with that than I did. At *The Simpsons,* it's a very different type of situation. You're just getting notes from Jim Brooks and Matt Groening, basically."

BURNING QUESTION

What is the secret of *The Simpsons'* success?

The true secret to *The Simpsons'* success is the valuable input of network executives.

We don't have any.

When it was greenlit, Jim Brooks decreed that no studio or network exec would be allowed anywhere near the show. When we record *The Simpsons,* any bum off the street is allowed to come in and watch. But the president of Fox is not allowed in. Until he gets fired and becomes a bum on the street. (Approximately 80 percent of L.A.'s homeless population is former network presidents.)

One time I was directing the actors on *The Simpsons* and the president of Fox came by with his little boy. The president said, "I know I'm not allowed in here . . . but can my son watch for a little bit?" And I said, "Sure. Fine."

The boy was very politely watching the show, and Jim Brooks came in and said, "Who's the kid?" I told him it was the network president's son. Jim got very angry—he didn't even want executives' kids in the room! And that's when I told a lie I'm not proud of: "Uh, Jim . . . he's deaf."

Who are network executives? People who meddle in every part of the creative process. People who get paid to turn junk into crap.

I first saw these guys back in the eighties. There were three executives who ran all of ABC. They would go from show to show to see if the producers were doing coke. And, if so, was it good and where could they get some?

Twenty years later, I was back at ABC doing another sitcom. Now I had eleven executives working full time on my show alone. They would bombard me with helpful suggestions like:

Does the rabbi have to be Jewish?

How do the zombies feel about being zombies?

Could you make Satan more likable?

And eleven executives is not the most I've seen. When you do a show with a big star, executives start multiplying like cockroaches (my apologies to cockroaches). My friend did a pilot for a red-hot comic, and every day he had to send copies of the script to forty-five executives. I scanned the list and told him, "Three of the people on this list are dead. Every day, you're sending scripts to three dead people."

He replied, "I wish more were."

And with all this help—a big star and forty-five mostly living executives giving their input—how did the show do? It never got past pilot.

As Jerry Seinfeld would ask, "Who are these people?" Network executives are largely M.B.A.s with no experience in writing or producing, telling writers and producers how to do their jobs. You must take their notes, no matter how moronic. And the number of moronic notes they've given over the years would fill a book.

I know this because there is such a book: It's called *A Martian Wouldn't Say That!* and it's ninety-six pages of actual studio notes. The title is something an executive said on the set of *My Favorite Martian*.

Of course, there's still plenty of great TV out there—not on the big networks, but on HBO, AMC, Netflix. These are places that hire creative people, then back off and let them do their jobs. When writer-director-actor-masturbator Louis C.K. pitched his brilliant show *Louie* to FX, they told him, "We'll give you $200,000 to make each episode—or $300,000 if you let us give you notes."

Louie said, "I'll take the two hundred grand."

CHAPTER FOURTEEN

DOING ANIMATED FILMS FOR CASH (NOT CREDIT)

Animated films can take years to make, giving producers endless chances to rethink, recast, revise, and test the film before audiences. The original screenwriter is often unavailable (or unwilling) to make these changes, so the work is done by some anonymous hack.

Meet the anonymous hack. I've done punch-up and rewrites on animated films too numerous to mention.

All right, I'll mention them: *Despicable Me* and *Despicable Me 2*, *Minions*, *The Secret Life of Pets*, all five of the *Ice Age* films, *The Lorax*, *Horton Hears a Who*, *Kung Fu Panda 3*, *Rio*, *Rio 2*, *Rango*, *Robots*, *Epic*, *Gnomeo and Juliet*, *Hop*, *Everyone's Hero*, and *The Simpsons Movie*. My films have a worldwide gross of $11 billion. I'm bigger than Pixar, baby!

I also wrote the "Ice Age Christmas Special." If you're wondering how you can set a Christmas special ten thousand years before Christ . . . well, you just do.

I'm a handyman, called in when things go wrong. Sometimes I'm sent a list of jokes in the script that need to be funnier. Other times they ask for a whole new scene to clarify a story or round out a character. Then there are the times they just send the whole script and say, "Save it!"

I contributed a lot to *Despicable Me,* including the final scene where the villain, Gru, reads a bedtime story. I also wrote every kid's favorite line, where Gru unveils his evil plan: "I fly to the moon, I shrink the moon, I grab the moon, I sit on the toilet!"

But my most lasting contribution was to *Despicable Me*'s Minions: I gave the little bastards names. Throughout the script, Gru would always refer to them collectively as "boys," but I thought it would be funny to address them each by name, since, to me, they were alike as a pile of little yellow Advils. In order to contrast their weirdness, I gave them bland white-guy names. I chose from the blandest white guys I know: *Simpsons* writers. I used the first names of staff members like Kevin Curran, Stewart Burns, Bob Bendetson, and about ten others.

None of this seemed like a big deal until the *Minions* movie came out years later. Each poster for the film featured a single Minion, with the slogan, "Meet Kevin," or "Meet Stewart," or "Meet Bob." I couldn't tell them apart, but the kids could. It's like how my father felt about the Beatles.

Often, rewriting can be frustrating work. Although filmmakers know they're in trouble and they're paying me to help, they're still reluctant to fix what's broken.

The producer of *Horton Hears a Who* came to me and said, "There's a line in this film that makes me sick. I literally want to vomit every time I hear it. Can you do better?" Write something better than an emetic? You bet!

I gave him twenty alternatives to the line, and yet, when I attended the premiere of the film, I saw that line was still in there! I swear I heard the producer barfing in the balcony.

The line, if you're curious, was something an imaginative child said about a clover: "My best friend, Thidwick, lives on that!" I did write a line that came after it: "In my world, everyone's a pony, and they all eat rainbows and poop butterflies." I tend to write a lot of toilet jokes for these films, and, by God, they always get in.

On the next film I worked on, no matter what I wrote, the script never changed. I tried to quit repeatedly, telling the producers, "You don't need to use my jokes, but you need to use somebody's." Each time, they begged me to stay, saying they really needed the work I was doing. When the film wrapped, I found out there were nineteen other writers working on the script at the same time. Nineteen!

When they were starting a sequel to this film, I said no thanks. Two years later, I got a heartfelt call from the producer, saying, "We're finishing the sequel, and it's just not working. It needs the Mike Reiss touch." (That's a phrase never used before or since.) He went on, "I know there's been some bad blood in the past, but we wondered if you might come on board and help us."

I was touched. I said, "I'd be happy to do it. I'll even do it for free." (That's another phrase never used before or since.) I went on, "But you know that long list of thanks at the end of every movie? Where you thank Dollar Rent A Car, and the state of Georgia, and the assistant studio nurse? Put me on the 'Thanks' list."

The producer called me back the next day. "No deal," he said.

I wrote the greatest joke of my career for *The Lorax*. In that film, and the Dr. Seuss book that inspired it, people are obsessively buying something called thneeds. There are billboards reading THNEED all over the film. So I suggested that at the end of the movie, the Lorax move the *N* in THNEED to the right, so it now reads . . . THE END.

Perfect, right? It's the kind of joke writers call a "find." Remember, the one out there waiting to be discovered?

The *Lorax* producer loved the joke, animated it, put it in the film, took it out of the film, and replaced it with nothing at all. Why? I'll never know.

For some reason, studios will use any excuse to avoid ever putting in a new joke. Here are some of the best excuses I've heard:

My three-year-old won't get it.

It won't translate into Portuguese.

That joke will lose us a hundred million in Korea alone. (NOTE: No film has ever grossed a hundred million in Korea.)

And the most popular excuse:

We can save it in animation.

Oh, that line. Cartoon directors believe they can make a bad joke work by adding a grace note after a failed punchline: a long pause; a character blinks; a fish tank bubbles; a bit of snow falls off a tree. You can see it all over *Gnomeo and Juliet,* a fine piece of family entertainment from Harvey Weinstein.

Former *Simpsons* director Jim Reardon bears this out. After he left our show, he went off to work on classic animated features, like *Zootopia, Wreck-It Ralph,* and *Wall-E.* (He cowrote the last one and got an Oscar nomination for his script.) I asked Reardon if he learned anything from his *Simpsons* experience. He said, "You taught me that if a joke doesn't work, cut it." He said other animators killed themselves trying to save a bit that just wasn't funny.

Why do studios hire consultants when they're so loath to use their work? I suppose it's like asking for advice. You're hoping the answer will be "Here's an easy fix to make everything all right," or even better, "Don't change a thing. You're perfect." Any input offered beyond that is not welcome at all.

Of all the films I've been a part of, the toughest job I ever had was on an animated film called *Everyone's Hero*. You don't remember it? It was about the bickering relationship between a baseball (Rob Reiner) and a bat (Whoopi Goldberg). That's why you don't remember it.

I spent six months writing snappy banter for these two:

BASEBALL: Suck my stitches.

BAT: Bite my knob.

That's about it.

When the movie came out, nobody in America saw it. Nobody in Europe saw it. The original director died before the film came out, so even he didn't see it. *Everyone's Hero* was no one's movie.

A few years later, my wife and I were visiting Iran. Why? Because our idea of a vacation is most people's idea of a hostage situation. If refugees want to get out of a place, we want to go there. Anyway . . . in every city and village in Iran, in every shop and market stall, vendors were selling bootleg DVDs of this film. One day, we climbed a mountain outside of Tehran; at the top of that mountain was a cave; and at the back of that cave was a blind Muslim cleric standing by a wooden table. He was selling two things: copies of the Koran and DVDs of *Everyone's Hero*.

This movie is the reason Iran hates us.

If working on that film was a forgettable experience, working on *Ice Age* was a remarkable one. The series was created by a brilliant woman named Lori Forte—I'd known her years before, when she was the network executive on *ALF*. Lori treats writers with respect, never piling them onto a project. There are only five or six of us who write all those films, and none of us mind that we're rewriting each other's work. And when a joke needs fixing, it gets fixed.

I like to think this has helped make *Ice Age* the most successful animated franchise of all time—bigger than *Toy Story* and *Shrek*. Weirdest of all, the biggest hit was the third one, *Ice Age: Dawn of the Dinosaurs.*

When I saw that title, I told the producer, "There were no dinosaurs in the Ice Age. They'd been dead for sixty-five million years."

The producer said, "Nobody knows that."

So I plugged away at the script for a year, occasionally dropping in dialogue like, "Why are there dinosaurs in the Ice Age?" and "I thought these guys were extinct."

Those lines always got cut. "Nobody knows that," the producer told me again.

Two weeks before the film came out, the studio had a test screening of the film. Ten minutes into the movie, a little boy shouted, "Why are there dinosaurs in the Ice Age?"

But the producers were right: none of this hurt the film. *Ice Age: Dawn of the Dinosaurs* was a success in America; overseas, it was the third-biggest film of all time, behind *Titanic* and *The Lord of the Rings: The Return of the King.*

When reporters asked why the movie was so successful, the filmmakers all had the same answer: "We have no friggin' idea." The best explanation I ever heard came during another one of my fun vacations: Ukraine. I'd gone to visit Chernobyl, for *Simpsons* research—yes, it's their hottest tourist attraction, in every sense of the word. Afterward, I went to a park in Kiev that was filled with statues of Scrat, the *Ice Age* squirrel who's always pursuing an acorn but never quite getting it. I asked a Ukrainian woman why they loved Scrat so much. She said, "He teaches children that life is hopeless."

From *Ice Age: Dawn of the Dinosaurs*: Sid the
sloth and the three eggs I named: Egbert, Shelly,
and Yoko.

CHAPTER FIFTEEN

THE SLEAZY, NASTY WORLD OF CHILDREN'S BOOKS

Something happened a few years ago that I couldn't believe: the Pope endorsed *The Simpsons*. Pope Benedict, the German pontiff who sort of resembled Mr. Burns, called our show the most Christian and moral show on television. It made me wonder if he'd ever actually seen the series. We'd just done an episode where Homer got sodomized by a giant panda. And it was our Christmas show.

The Simpsons had clearly come a long way. When the show premiered in 1989, it was condemned by church groups across America—until someone pointed out that the Simpsons were the only family on TV that actually went to church.

Our first season was also panned by First Lady Barbara Bush, who called the show "the dumbest thing I have ever seen." (Hey lady, look at your kids!)

I took all this criticism very personally, thinking I was bringing about America's moral decay. So I decided to write children's books. This was a stretch for me, because I hate children. But, Dr.

Seuss hated children. So did Hans Christian Andersen. Lewis Carroll *loved* children in a way that's illegal in forty-eight states. (I mentioned this in a lecture, and someone asked, "What are the two states where it's okay?" That's how I met R. Kelly.)

Since then, I've published nearly twenty children's books. Choosing my favorite would be like picking which of my children I love the most: there are some I like much more than others, and a few I can't stand at all. My best book—the sweetest, the most educational, and the most inspiring—is called *The Boy Who Looked Like Lincoln*.

The idea for the book came to me in a dream one night. It's the story of an eight-year-old who looks exactly like Honest Abe: he's got the hat, he's got the beard, he's got the wart. Other children make fun of him, so his parents send him to a camp for kids who look like things: there's a boy who looks like a frog, a girl who looks like a toaster, and four kids who look like Mount Rushmore. In the end, he learns that it's not important what you look like; what matters is who you are. This doesn't explain why supermodels make so much more than schoolteachers, but what the hell, it's just a kids' book. I hoped it would provide comfort to ugly children everywhere. And there are a lot of ugly kids out there. I know. I've been to Chuck E. Cheese's.

The book was beautifully illustrated by David Catrow, a man who's done seven of my books. Our partnership is like a marriage: no communication whatsoever. I've never met the guy, never talked on the phone with him—I don't even know his email address. Publishers keep authors and illustrators completely separated, and this may be a good thing. Another artist once slipped me some of his sketches for our upcoming book. I told him I loved everything in the story except the little boy—he looked effeminate and he always had his mouth open in an astonished O. "Frankly, the kid looks like a gay sex doll," I said.

"That's my son," he replied.

I was very proud of *The Boy Who Looked Like Lincoln* right up to the moment the hate mail started pouring in. A school in Springfield, Massachusetts, wrote to tell me they'd removed my book from their library. A minister in Iowa burned the book in his church parking lot. (This is not as bad as it sounds—before they can burn it, they've got to buy it.) Finally, the Texas State Board of Education banned my book.

I was shocked—*shocked*—to learn that Texas had books. Lee Harvey Oswald knew it was safe to shoot Kennedy from the Texas School Book Depository because no Texan would willingly walk into a warehouse full of books.

The Texas ruling explained the anger readers felt toward this book, claiming that it contained "profanity" and "sexual content." What? Where? On the last page, the boy who looks like Lincoln hopes he can help his little brother, Dick, a baby who, it turns out, looks exactly like Richard Nixon. But the Texas censors assumed the baby was named Dick because he looked like . . . well, you get it. They couldn't tell our thirty-seventh president from male gonads.

Now, I'll admit that Dick Nixon did resemble a dong: his phallic nose, his testicular jowls . . . it could be why we remain simultaneously repulsed and fascinated by the man. But Penguin Books has not stayed in business for more than a century by ending children's books with full frontal male nudity. The baby in my book really was supposed to be Dick Nixon. He had a five o'clock shadow, he was waving two Vs for victory . . . the kid had a little tape recorder, for crying out loud.

To recap: the Pope loves *The Simpsons*, yet it's my sweet children's book that's getting censored. And who are the people making these decisions? That's not a rhetorical question—no one knows who the people are in Texas who decide what children can read. But I've figured out three things about the people who banned *The Boy Who Looked Like Lincoln*:

1. They have no sense of history.

2. They have no sense of humor.

3. They have filthy fucking minds.

The offending Nixon.

Did Steve Martin Rip Me Off?

The toughest part about getting a children's book published is that you're competing with celebrity authors. There's Julie Andrews and Judy Collins, Kathie Lee Gifford and Jamie Lee Curtis, Johns Travolta and Lithgow, Queen Noor of Jordan and Sarah Ferguson. God help me, I'm fighting for shelf space with a queen and a duchess. And Madonna. Since stores arrange books by the author's last name, I find my work—by Reiss—sandwiched between books by Carl Reiner and LeAnn Rimes.

What bothers me is that so many of these books aren't exactly books. Jerry Seinfeld's and Jay Leno's stories are actually excerpts from their stand-up routines. David Byrne's children's book is just the lyrics from one of his songs, as is Neil Sedaka's.

Then there's Steve Martin's first children's book, 2010's *Late for School*, the most charming book I've read since my 2003 book *Late for School*.

Both tell the story of a boy facing adventure on a mad dash for school. Both are written in verse. Both have the boy jumping over a pool. (It rhymes with "school.") The biggest difference is that my book's final twist has the boy arriving at school right on time, and then—spoiler alert!—realizing it's Sunday. In Steve Martin's book, it's Saturday.

I'm not saying Steve ripped off my book, or even knew it existed. Steve Martin is a brilliant comedian, playwright, and novelist. I'm thrilled that we had the exact same idea, and that I had it seven years earlier.

There is an upside to the celebrity domination of kiddie books. Recently a publishing house called me in a panic. They had a children's book contract with an African American superstar, and his manuscript was unusable—even by celebrity standards. (I can't tell you his name, but he can play anything from a nutty professor to a Beverly Hills cop.) They asked me—a Jewish kid from suburban Connecticut—to write a book about growing up as a poor black kid in the slums of New York. And they needed it the next day.

I informed them huffily, "A children's book is not a fast-food hamburger and I am not McDonald's."

They said they'd pay me ten thousand dollars.

I said, "You want fries with that?"

If you still don't believe that the children's book business is sleazier than network TV, I submit this: I was commissioned to write a children's book by a New York department store, though I'm forbidden to say which one.

The store was doing a big promotion on cashmere and wanted a storybook from the point of view of the goat who lived in the store.

"One more thing," they added. "You won't get writing credit—the goat will." I didn't mind—it was a work for hire, and I cranked it out pretty quickly. The store loved it too, except for my original title: *Saks and the Single Goat*. Whoops! What a giveaway!

The book came out beautifully and was sold at all the stores in the chain. My name wasn't on it—instead it said it was written by the goat . . . "and Terry Shuster." Terry Shuster? Who the hell was that?

He was the vice president of the store. He even dedicated the book to his kids. At least I think they're his kids. Maybe someone else did that work for him, too.

CHAPTER SIXTEEN

GAY FOR PAY

Okay, I'll be perfectly blunt here: my favorite project I've ever worked on isn't *The Simpsons, The Critic,* or any of those great animated films—it's a little web series I created called *Queer Duck* (tagline: *He can't even FLY straight!*).

The show was born in 2000, in the great dot-com boom (and bust). My friends had started a company called Icebox, and it would feature a new online cartoon every day. The company was literally ahead of its time—these were the days of dial-up internet, and it took twenty minutes to download each three-minute cartoon.

Icebox offered no pay, just complete creative freedom, and most *Simpsons* writers jumped at that. Everyone got to write about topics that obsessed them: Jeff Martin did a series about Elvis and Jack Nicklaus solving mysteries; Dana Gould wrote about the Beach Boys' domineering father Murry Wilson; and I dusted off a sketch I'd written in high school but never used: *Hard Drinkin' Lincoln.* This featured a snockered Abraham Lincoln at Ford's Theatre loudly heckling the actors; when Abe finally gets shot, the audience cheers.

Giant Abe Lincoln goes Godzilla on D.C. in *Hard Drinkin' Lincoln*.

Hard Drinkin' Lincoln was so popular, *South Park* ripped it off. That's a bold claim, but here's the case. I wrote an episode called "Abezilla" where the statue in the Lincoln Memorial comes to life and goes on a rampage in Washington, D.C. To kill him, the army creates a giant John Wilkes Booth. Crazy idea, right? Six months later, *South Park* (which shared a writer with Icebox) did the same story on its "Super Best Friends" episode. You can see both clips on YouTube—it's pretty blatant. I don't think it was an intentional theft: things like this happen when you crank out a whole episode in just a week, as *South Park* does. (It takes *The Simpsons* thirty-six weeks, minimum.) Anyway, imitation is the sincerest form of felony.

I followed up *Hard-Drinkin' Lincoln* with a pet project called *Queer Duck*.

Queer Duck was a cartoon about a gay duck (surprise) and his gay animal pals Openly Gator, Bi-Polar Bear, Oscar Wildcat, Truman Coyote, Keangaru Reeves, Ricky Marlin, and the questionably tasteful HIV Possum and Patient Zebra.

Queer Duck made history as the first openly gay cartoon character. Now, I say *openly* gay because *all* cartoon characters are kind of gay: Bugs Bunny kisses Elmer Fudd on the mouth, Snagglepuss is theatrical, Daffy Duck has a lisp. Tweety Pie *is* Truman Capote.

The Pink Panther? *C'mon.*

Donald Duck is a character right out of gay porn: he wears a sailor suit but no pants.

And Woody Woodpecker's name is a euphemism for Erectiony Erection Penis.

The Simpsons, of course, has its gay characters. But Marge's sister Patty didn't come out of the closet till five years after Queer Duck. Not that she surprised anyone. Homer's reaction was "Patty's gay? Here's another bomb. I like beer!" As for Smithers, it took him twenty-seven years to finally admit he was gay. Just like my cousin Lee.

Queer Duck made it big— literally. He once made the cover of *Time Out New York.*

DAN CASTELLANETA ON ICEBOX

"I know Mike did things for the Internet: *Hard Drinkin' Lincoln* and *Queer Duck*. That's his real dark sense of humor. He just goes there. He doesn't worry about the line. He finds out about the line *after* he says what he says. I was listening to a podcast he was doing, and Gilbert Gottfried said, 'Lemme guess, you're Jewish?' And Mike says, 'Yes. I made a living modeling for hate literature.' That's about as dark as you can go."

As silly and raunchy as it is, I created *Queer Duck* as an act of conscience. I read two troubling articles in the year 2000: One reported that Colorado had barred homosexuals from teaching in public schools, the other that there were no gay characters on TV. *None.* This was before *Glee* and *Will & Grace* and Anderson Cooper and Rush Limbaugh. (*"Oh, my God! He just outed Rush Limbaugh!"*)

So I decided to redress these wrongs the only way I knew how: through cartoons.

The title came from a saying I used to hear as a kid (mostly about me): "That boy is a *queer duck!*" It didn't imply homosexuality. A queer duck was just a weirdo. If the phrase had been "queer mole," my cartoon would've been about a mole. (By the way, if you develop a queer mole, see a doctor.)

People ask, "How do you write *Queer Duck*? You're not gay. You're bi."

I'm not gay. No, no. A thousand times no.

Three times, yes, but I was drunk. The first time.

Seriously, I'm not gay. But I *am* Jewish, which is kind of the same thing. We've both been oppressed for centuries. By our mothers.

In truth, I did have some concerns about the project at first. I even told the folks at Icebox that if this ended up being perceived as gay-bashing in any way, I'd pull the plug. I was doing this *for* gay people. I was giving them their own Bugs Bunny.

I even offered to turn the whole thing over to a gay cartoon writer, of which there are many. But Icebox said it would be fine, and just asked that we use a gay actor to voice Queer Duck.

The first person who came in to audition was Scott Thompson, the openly gay member of the hilarious *Kids in the Hall* comedy troupe and a mainstay of Garry Shandling's *The Larry Sanders Show*.

I was very pleased to meet Scott . . . until he started berating me. Loudly. It embodied all my worst fears about the project: How insensitive the script was, how dare I presume to write it . . .

He chewed me out for twenty solid minutes, ending with a comment about my obviously Jewish appearance and asking how I would like it if someone were to do something like this about Jews. *Oy vey.*

And then . . . Scott Thompson proceeded to audition. He was even funny, but his reading sounded . . . hostile. (Two days later a friend saw Scott do stand-up—he was still angry, and his whole act was a tirade against this big-nosed guy doing a gay cartoon.)

Luckily for me, he was the last person to ever complain about *Queer Duck*. The next actor to audition was the buoyant and flamboyant Jim J. Bullock, who captured all the joy of the character. He got the part; it was an easy decision.

The supporting cast was mostly very talented people I'd worked with before: Tress MacNeille from *The Simpsons,* Maurice LaMarche and Nick Jameson from *The Critic,* and even a veteran of *Homeboys in Outer Space*: Kevin Michael Richardson.

The show was launched on October 11, 2000—National Coming Out Day—and immediately broke the dial-up internet. Viewership on Icebox.com spiked 400 percent, and the website crashed. Clearly the show filled a void. Two days later, a reporter called to interview me—from Germany!

I knew people were loving it, because there was a message board under the videos saying things like, "Oh, thank God! Finally a cartoon for me!" And when, every once in a while, we *would* receive a stupid comment like "I hate this gay shit!," I just thought, *All right! If I make a homophobe angry, that's like making a homosexual happy!*

One day, someone posted, "I wish this cartoon was around when I was thirteen. It would have made my life so much easier." To this day, that's the best review I ever got in my life.

Queer Duck became such a hit that it made the jump to the Showtime network (airing after *Queer as Folk*) and, unknown to me, was shown weekly on Britain's Channel 4. In 2005, a poll of Channel 4 viewers named *Queer Duck* "One of the 100 Greatest Cartoons of All Time." (Now, mind you, England is the world's only exclusively gay country. Britain's an island—it's like a big gay cruise that doesn't go anywhere.)

The response to *Queer Duck* has always been positive. I have a shelf of awards from gay groups. At least I think they're awards. Many vibrate. GLAAD endorsed the series and even Howard Stern praised it. There's the full spectrum right there: from GLAAD to Howard Stern.

"I've never gotten any email or heard of someone who was offended," my amazingly talented director, Xeth Feinberg, said. "It seemed quite the opposite, actually. I'm surprised. I was expecting, 'You're insulting!' But I never got feedback like that."

The media opportunities and interviews rolled in, and, at first, I kept my mouth shut about being straight. In the beginning, when journalists would come over to interview me, I would hide my wedding pictures and lock my wife in the bedroom.

But then I came out of the closest (and let Denise out of the bedroom), and everyone was fine with my not being gay. When the *New York Times* wrote about it, they said, "*Queer Duck* was created by Mike Reiss . . . who is straight." My father loved that—he never believed *anything* unless it was in the *New York Times*.

How popular was Queer Duck? Well, he made appearances in two Gay Pride parades. One in Los Angeles . . .

. . . and one in Springfield! In the 2002 *Simpsons* episode "Jaws Wired Shut," a giant Queer Duck balloon flew over Springfield's gay parade. Sadly, the scene was dropped, putting Queer Duck in that elite category of Celebrity Guests Cut from *Simpsons* Episodes for No Friggin' Reason with the likes of SCTV's brilliant Catherine O'Hara, John Cusack, John Turturro, and Aaron Sorkin.

In 2005, I made a *Queer Duck* movie for Paramount Pictures. *Variety* called it the best animated film of the year (in the same year Brad Bird's Academy Award–winning *Ratatouille* came out). I showed the film in Germany and the audience laughed for seventy-five straight minutes, thereby doubling the total amount of time Germans have ever laughed.

You can still buy the movie on DVD from Amazon: you get the full film, the original Icebox shorts, and a making-of documentary.

Here's what you *don't* get:

I had a song in the movie during which all the gay animals are going to Disneyland. They sing "*Let's call Tom Cruise . . . What can we lose?*" Paramount made me take that out, because Tom Cruise sues people who call him gay. All right. So I changed the line to, "*Forget Tom Cruise . . . Call him gay, and he sues.*" Paramount made me take *that* line out, too. So I told this story in the making-of documentary on the DVD. I said, "You can call anyone in this world gay except for Tom Cruise." Paramount told me to take that out, too. When I asked why, they gave me a very Orwellian response:

"*It's against Paramount policy to discuss Paramount policy.*"

Then the editor of the documentary had an idea—he obscured my lips and futzed the audio in the making-of doc so that I would say, "You can call anyone in this world gay except for [MURBLE BURBLE MURBLE]."

Paramount made me take *that* out, too. When I asked why, they said, "Because everyone *knows* you're talking about Tom Cruise."

CHAPTER SEVENTEEN

WRITING FOR HUMANS AGAIN!

I spent the first eight years of my career writing for real live people (if you count ALF and Joan Rivers). However, "once you go toon, you won't be back soon," as no one ever said. It is very liberating to write for cartoon characters because they don't take the jokes personally. Marge's sister can say, "Am I wrong, or did it just get fatter in here?" and Dan Castellaneta's feelings are not hurt. Cruel lines fly freely on *The Simpsons* and our actors never take it to heart.

Only once did a *Simpsons* actor resist a line. Hank Azaria didn't want to record Moe's response to a prank phone caller: "I'm a stupid moron with an ugly face and a big butt and my butt smells and . . . I like to kiss my own butt." But eventually he did it!

Contrast this with *Roseanne*, a great TV series about an elephant married to a hippopotamus. For nine seasons, Roseanne insulted everyone in sight, but nobody ever responded, "Shut up, fatso." No one ever seemed to notice her weight. Why? Because Roseanne was a human being. And it was her show.

So, it was with some trepidation that I went back to the world of writing for human beings. The results were . . . mixed.

Jokes for Bob Hope? Nope, the Pope!

I wrote jokes for Johnny Carson, the Pope of late-night TV. But I also wrote gags for Pope Francis, the Johnny Carson of the Catholic Church. It started with my friend Ed Conlon, who's from a big Irish family: his aunts are all nuns, his uncles are priests; his mother's a nun; his father is also a nun. I was at his St. Patrick's Day party when I met Father Andrew, the Friar Tuck–ish head of Catholic charities for New York. "You wanna see the Pope's app?" he asked. At least, I think he said "app."

It was called Joke with the Pope, and had videos of celebrities and nobodies telling jokes to Pope Francis. Through some mechanism I've never understood, this would benefit orphans in Cambodia and Venezuela. I could just picture the poor waifs saying, "I sure liked that joke George Lopez told the Pope, but I'd still rather have parents. Or pants."

Father Andrew emailed me at midnight, later that week: "We need a joke for Al Roker to tell the Pope. It needs to be about religion and weather and it must be clean." I came up with this: "The California drought is so bad people in Napa are asking the Pope to change the wine into water."

No one thinks that joke is funny—they always say it's "cute." CUTE, I realized, is an acronym for Completely Unable To Entertain. But the joke made it to the app, so every few nights, Father Andrew would email me, requesting jokes for Mayor Bloomberg, Conan O'Brien, David Copperfield, and on and on. There are eight hundred million Catholics on earth, but somehow the church had to bother me. I was a Jew writing jokes for the Pope. For free. That's two sins. Still, Jesus relied on Jewish writers for his Gospels, too.

When the project finally wrapped, the charity threw itself a very lavish party. And, to my complete surprise, I was presented with a plaque from Pope Francis, naming me "a Missionary of Joy."

"Well," I quipped to the clergymen assembled, "this isn't the first time a priest has put a man in the missionary position."

Next time, they should pay me.

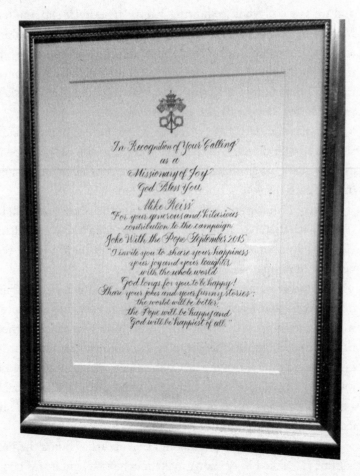

See? I really did win an award from Pope Francis. I wouldn't have believed it, either.

A Half-Life in the Theater

After thirty-five years of working movies and TV, I started writing plays. Why? Because after a while you get tired of earning money and having people see your work.

I fell into theater by accident. My wife and I were in London, and we saw a playhouse showing *Waiting for Godot* starring Ian McKellen and Michael Gambon (that's Gandalf and Dumbledore to you). The show was sold out, but we decided to stand on the ticket line, hoping for someone to cancel their tickets. We waited for two hours but never got in. "Couldn't this be a play?" I asked my wife. "*Waiting for 'Waiting for Godot'*?"

My wife said, "No," but I wrote it anyhow. I even got my friend's sister, a theater director, to stage the show. The one-act play opens as Dave arrives at a theater showing *Waiting for Godot* and it's sold out. He calls his wife as another man listens:

"Honey, I couldn't get tickets. Is there another show you want to see? What's that? 'Go fuck yourself'? It sounded like you said . . . *Go Fuck Yourself.*" Dave explains to the other man: "That's the new David Mamet play."

The opening line got an enormous laugh, much better than it deserved—and I was hooked. Theater was easy, the audiences were generous, and the actors did every line I wrote. I learned this during my first full-length play, *I'm Connecticut,* which won every award you can win. In Connecticut. The play featured a tough-talking Massachusetts guy: "In Boston, we call a milkshake a frappe. A frappe. What is that? It's 'crap' with a 'fff'.' And we call ice cream sprinkles jimmies. Who the hell is Jimmy?"

Every night, the actor would end that speech, "*Who's* the hell is Jimmy?" I liked it—it didn't make much sense, but it was good character.

When the play finally closed, I checked the script—it was a typo. In theater, the actors do your typos.

My Rep in Ruins

After visiting half the countries on earth, I was able to put my world travel to good use: in 2009, I wrote a sweet little romantic comedy film called *My Life in Ruins*. It was about a bus tour of Greece, and had big laughs, gorgeous scenery, and a simple message: don't judge others too harshly.

One critic called it "execrable."

I was fully prepared for bad reviews, but nothing quite this vicious. *Sledge Hammer!* star David Rasche, who'd been in a critically trashed play, tried to spin it: "'Execrable' can mean 'deserving to be excreted.' See? 'Deserving.' That's good! Or it can mean 'of poorest quality.' Okay, see? 'Quality.' That is also very good!"

I was surprised because my film was the highest-testing movie in Fox Searchlight history. Audiences liked it more than, say, *Little Miss Sunshine* and *Slumdog Millionaire*. But not the critics. They called it "one big fat Greek disaster"; "wretched"; "thuddingly bad"; "a film that will kill Greek tourism"; and "a steaming pile of stereotypes and sitcomery, a pathetic excuse for a comedy." That last review sent my wife to a sickbed for three days, with what Victorian doctors used to call "the vapors."

Roger Ebert, who'd guest-starred on my show *The Critic,* called me an imbecile. Other critics singled me out, calling me "an idiot" and "sub-literate." Now, I opened the film with an allusion to Voltaire—a sign reads PANGLOSS TOURS: "THE BEST OF ALL POSSIBLE WORLDS." In *Candide,* Dr. Pangloss utters these optimistic words before his group sets out on an utterly disastrous journey. Just like the tourists in my film! Get it? The critics didn't. Not one caught the allusion. Otherwise, they'd have called me a "sub-literate moron who reads Voltaire."

We all have to deal with criticism in this world. But only people in entertainment have to deal with critics. You may get a performance review at work that reads, "Jim's efficiency in processing claims is down 11 percent; needs improvement." If it read, "Jim's work recalls a drooling monkey who can't tell a banana from a ballpoint pen"—well, you'd have grounds for a lawsuit.

I can't speak for all writers, but for me, bad reviews hurt. I can still quote you every nasty write-up I've gotten over the past thirty-five years. Why shouldn't I? I try my best on everything I do, and my works are my babies. I don't want Manohla Dargis coming to my home and saying, "Mike Reiss's newest offering, *Mike Jr.,* is a babbling, bloated sequel to the thoroughly unpleasant original. Avoid this soggy diaper of a child."

My movie was panned and my book was banned. I needed to retreat to a safe space. It was time to head back to *The Simpsons.*

CHAPTER EIGHTEEN

BACK TO THE OLD TIRE FIRE

I'd spent a few years away from *The Simpsons*, dabbling in different projects, and in that time I had the pleasure of watching the show each week, as a fan. I no longer knew what was coming in every episode, which was a treat. Most importantly, it solidified what I had believed all along: *The Simpsons* was great! In fact, it may have been better without me.

Then, in season 12, the wonderful showrunner, Mike Scully, called and asked if I wanted to return to the series one day a week, as a consultant. I jumped at the chance. Scully had been the Henry Ford of the series, streamlining production, delegating authority, and turning *The Simpsons* into something it had never been before: a nine-to-five job. Up to that point, the show's hours had always been insane, and writers quit the second they had a chance.

It was great to be working with Al Jean again—he'd gone back to *The Simpsons* in 1997, right after the cancellation of *Teen Angel*. But for the most part, I was working with a roomful of strangers. These were all very talented writers, but they weren't a group of old friends, like the original staff. It was no longer collegial—it was like . . . high school. There was gossip, cliques, and an awful lot of backbiting.

At times, this nastiness would leach into the show. Like when Bart strangled Homer with a phone cord and beat him unconscious with the receiver. Or when Milhouse's father had his arm cut off by a piano wire. Or when Mr. Burns threw fish guts at orphans on Christmas. The shows were always funny, but they also could get pretty dark.

I wasn't having fun and thought about quitting. But eventually, things straightened themselves out. The malcontents quit and the jerks got fired. Everyone else mellowed—the show has that effect on people. It's such a great job, it's hard to be bitter. And I loved working one day a week. I moved to New York City twelve years ago, but I still fly to L.A. every Wednesday, put in a day's work at *The Simpsons,* and then get the hell out of town.

And then a project came along that sucked me back full time . . .

. . . The Simpsons Movie

In 1992, we screened rough animation—the animatic—of "Kamp Krusty" for James L. Brooks: Jim got very excited. "This is it! This could be *The Simpsons Movie*! You just need to stretch it a little!"

A movie? "Kamp Krusty" was barely an episode! At seventeen minutes long it was several minutes too short to air. The song "Hail to Thee, Kamp Krusty" was added later just to reach minimum length.

But the idea of doing a *Simpsons* movie kept coming up over the next decade. The producers always fought it. Why would anyone pay to see a show they get for free on TV every day?

And what could we show people that they hadn't seen already?

The answer: Bart's wiener. But I'm getting ahead of myself.

One day, fifteen seasons into the series, Fox showed us market research that said people wanted a *Simpsons* movie more than anything else. More than another *Harry Potter*. More than another *Star Wars*.

So we sat down for a writers' meeting to discuss the movie we'd been avoiding for a dozen years. We cracked the plot in three hours. The whole movie came out of that meeting: Homer gets a pig; Springfield gets polluted by pig crap; the government puts Springfield under a dome; the Simpsons flee to Alaska. It was that easy.

At the end of the meeting, Matt Groening said, "Remember— all of this is a secret."

I thought he meant the *plot* of the movie.

A few weeks later, I was speaking at a college in Oklahoma. A student asked if we were ever going to do a *Simpsons* movie. "Yes, we are," I said coyly, "but I can't tell you the plot. That's a secret!"

That night, I was in my hotel room watching CNN. A crawl went by at the bottom: MIKE REISS ANNOUNCES SIMPSONS MOVIE.

That's when I realized that the plot wasn't a secret. The whole damn movie was!

When I went back to work the next day, everyone at Fox was mad at me. A whole multinational corporation wanted to kill me. Matt Groening's first words to me were "Well, you just had to tell everybody . . ."

The studio had planned an elaborate teaser campaign to promote the film. For two years, you were going to see cryptic yellow billboards with the message "It's Coming . . ." Instead, I had blown the secret at Oklahoma State University.

It is a tribute to the kindness of Matt Groening and Jim Brooks that I didn't lose my job. That incident should have gotten me fired.

Instead, this book will get me fired.

Jim and Matt assembled an amazing staff to write the movie: two of our most prolific writers (John Swartzwelder and Jon Vitti);

one of our most esteemed (George Meyer); and four guys who had run the show in the past (Mike Scully, David Mirkin, Al Jean, and me). It was the most focused, talented roomful of writers I'd ever worked with. We started work every morning at ten A.M. sharp, no stragglers. And everyone concentrated on the job—the writers never went off on time-wasting tangents, no matter how hard I pushed them. We worked out the film's story, scene by scene, then divided it into seven sections. Each of us went home to write one twenty-page chunk.

We met up again two weeks later to lash together this 140-page Frankenstein of a script. To everyone's amazement, it read well—the movie worked. We got together as a group, polishing the script. I thought we had something perfect by our fifth draft.

What you saw in theaters was our 166th draft. It seems to be a rule of filmmaking that you never stop working till you run out of time. Almost every day we'd produce a new draft and shred a hundred copies of the old one. To write a film with an environmental message, we must have killed every tree in British Columbia.

And yet, for all that hard work, what's the only thing anyone remembers from *The Simpsons Movie*?

Spider-Pig, Spider-Pig
Does whatever a spider-pig does . . .

That's the kind of joke you write when you're high.
And we did.
As simple and dumb as it is, somehow it caught the public's fancy. It even became the number one ringtone in France! ("*Spider-cochon, spider-cochon . . .*")
I wrote another song for the film—a rousing tribute to the state of Alaska. I got the job because I was the only one on staff who'd actually been to Alaska. (I hated the place—the people are surly

and the mosquitoes are enormous. And vice versa.)

Here's my Alaska song, available to the public for the first time.

HOMER (sing-speaking):
New Englanders are snobby twerps
And southerners are lazy
Midwesterners are toothless jerks
The whole West Coast is crazy . . .
Delaware, you're well aware,
Is sucky as Kentucky . . .

BART: Uh, Homer? The song?

HOMER (rousing singing):
There is no state so great
In the lower forty-eight
As Alaska!

BARFLIES:
As Alaska!

HOMER:
You can cruise, drink brews,
And even meet some Jews
In Alaska!

JEWISH COUPLE (THE ICEBERGS):
In Elaskeh!

HOMER:
We can make our home in Fairbanks or Nome
It sure beats being trapped in a dome

BART/LISA:
Homer, we are friggin' bored

HOMER:
Duly noted and ignored!
I spell it A-L-A-S-S
K-A-H . . .

LISA:
Well, more or less . . .

HOMER:
This is the land I love the best
Oklahooooo-ma! (BEAT)
I mean Alasss-ka!

That song got cut from the movie. But then a lot of stuff got cut: the real Erin Brockovich recorded a guest voice. And we'd written cameos for Al Gore, Sean Penn, Russell Crowe, and the cast of *The View*. None of it's in the final film.

One of my favorite jokes got changed—I think it was George Meyer's line. Bart has been arrested for skateboarding naked, at Homer's goading. Homer shows up to get him and brings only a shirt. "You didn't bring my pants!" Bart cries.

Homer replies, "Who am I, Bill Blass?"

I loved that joke because it shows how blissfully out of touch Homer is. It's like when he guessed that Bart's favorite movie star was Steve McQueen.

Years later I was watching *The Simpsons Movie* on an airplane—it was showing on a little monitor mounted on an inch-wide stalk. They got to my favorite line, where Bart demands Homer give him pants.

Homer replies, "Who am I, Tommy Bahama?"

Tommy Bahama?

It may be a better joke—certainly it's hipper. But I missed Bill Blass. I didn't realize how angry I was until my wife caught me strangling the stalk the monitor was on.

Here's my best contribution to *The Simpsons Movie*. It's a sight gag: As the giant dome is being lowered over Springfield, it looks like the end of the world. Some people run out of a bar into a church. Others run out of a church into a bar.

All right, it doesn't read funny. But many people say it's their favorite thing in the movie (after that stupid Spider-Pig . . .). Film critic David Edelstein called it a joke so rich in meaning you could write a master's thesis on it. And you know how funny master's theses are.

One day, I met Garry Trudeau, creator of *Doonesbury,* one of my comedy heroes. He mentioned how much he loved that joke.

"I wrote that," I said.

Trudeau looked at me with deep respect. "That's the greatest three seconds in comedy history," he said.

"That's what my wife called our wedding night," I cracked.

And suddenly he lost all respect for me.

The Simpsons Movie came out in 2007 and became the second-most successful 2-D animated film in history, after *The Lion King* (up yours, Simba). The critics were happy and, more amazingly, the fans were happy, and we all agreed, "Let's never, ever do that again."

But just as couples have a second baby once they forget what a miserable time-suck the first one was, I'm sure we'll make another *Simpsons* movie. And then another one. And then another one.

I think we'll keep making *Simpsons* movies until we make a really rotten one.

Then we'll make two more.

You know, like *Shrek*.

My pitch, not that anyone asked, is to make the next *Simpsons* movie live-action. For example, we've looked all over to find an actor as bald as Homer Simpson and just as stupid. And then God gave us Vin Diesel.

For Flanders, I recommend *Fargo*'s William H. Macy. In fact, one of our writers met Macy at a party. When he heard my friend worked for *The Simpsons,* Macy apparently said, "If one more goddamn person tells me I should play Ned Flanders, I'm gonna strangle him."

William H. Macy, check.

And Tom Cruise would be surprisingly good as Smithers. Not that I'm calling Tom gay . . .

THE TRAILER YOU NEVER SAW

I wrote this song as a trailer for *The Simpsons Movie*. It was never used. Dammit.

Why Is Every Movie a TV Show?

Homer leaves Springfield's Aztec Theater—he passes posters for several movies based on TV shows. He sings a bouncy march like "Seventy-Six Trombones" or "Hey, Look Me Over." (Except for Smithers's lines, all dialogue is sung.)

HOMER:
Why is every movie a TV show?
How the hell can they charge me eight bucks?
I like it at home when it's a free show
But when I have to pay for it, it sucks! Sucks! SUCKS!

BURNS:
Why make motion pictures from the boob tube?
Not a bloody one of them is good!
Why'd they make a talkie out of F Troop?

SMITHERS (spoken):
They didn't, sir.

BURNS:
Well, they should!

SMITHERS (spoken):
I'll make some calls.

EXT. ANDROID'S DUNGEON - DAY
Comic Book Guy stands in *Star Trek* garb.

COMIC BOOK GUY (sweetly):
I saw Star Trek *one through eight*
And every one was great

Except Star Trek V: The Final Frontier *directed by Mr.*
    William Shatner—
(GROWING ANGER)
    Which was the worst Star Trek movie ever!

Comic Book Guy steps into the street and joins an angry mob, wielding pipes, boards with nails, etc. Homer leads the pack.

HOMER:
Let's kill all the Hollywood producers
Before they make another Scooby-Doo
'Cause TV shows become such rotten movies

MARGE:
I liked The Fugitive—

HOMER (happily):
Me too!

The mob transforms into a festive marching band, still led by Homer. They have colorful banners for *The Fugitive*.

CROWD:
The Fugitive! The Fugitive!

MARGE:
It was an Oscar-winning hit!

BART:
Remember when that man
Jumped right off that dam?

HOMER:
Remember when—
(THINKS)
    —Well, that was about it.

The parade suddenly loses steam—the band music dies out sourly.

ANGLE ON LISA

LISA:
Movies were once turned into TV shows
That gave us the classic series M*A*S*H

Our Barbershop Quartet, the Be Sharps, appears.

BARNEY:
But when a TV show becomes a movie

APU:
You get Flintstones

SKINNER:
You get Dragnet

BE SHARPS (long harmony):
You get tra-a-a-ash!

Big rousing finish.

HOMER:
You get a disgrace
Like Lost in Space
How long till they give us Will & Grace?

CROWD:
You get miscast mishmash
Flashy rehashed trash!

They hold a big pose. WIDEN TO SEE they are being filmed by a camera crew.

DIRECTOR:
Cut! Print! That's a wrap!

ANNOUNCER (V.O.):
The Simpsons Movie. Coming soon.

THE TAG

The last minute or two of *The Simpsons,* after our final commercial break, is known as "the tag"—in other words, an unsightly object that can and should be removed. The show went twenty years without having a tag before Fox decided we needed one.

Anything goes in a *Simpsons* tag. Sometimes we wrap up a dangling plot thread, sometimes it's a complete non sequitur. A few times, it's even been a scene cut from the middle of the show; it wasn't good enough for act 2, but it's good enough for act 4.

Some tags are truly inspired, some are just crap to fill things out. You can decide which this one is.

CHAPTER NINETEEN

IT NEVER ENDS . . .

Five years ago, *The Simpsons* released its first mobile game. We titled it *The Simpsons: Tapped Out*, a double entendre: the game involves tapping, but also ponders whether the show was losing creative steam . . .

But, the game went on to become the most downloaded app in the country.

That same year, we were nominated for an Oscar for our Maggie Simpson animated short "The Longest Daycare." And we made TV history three times in the year 2016. We opened one episode with a virtual reality couch gag—a four-minute immersive trip to "The Planet of the Couches." We closed another show with something that had never been attempted: improv animation. Homer, voiced by Dan Castellaneta, took questions live on the air, which we animated in real time. Finally, we took a stab at topical humor, speed-animating the Trump short "3 A.M." for YouTube; it got twelve million views. *The Simpsons* is a really old dog with some really new tricks.

We're about to start our thirtieth season, the longest-running series in prime-time history . . . by a decade. *Gunsmoke* lasted twenty years, *Lassie* did nineteen, *Ozzie and Harriet* went fourteen seasons . . . it's a little embarrassing what boring shows we're competing with. We're still one of Fox's top-rated series. We're a hit in seventy-one countries. There's a new *Simpsons* movie in the works—it's always in the works.

So we're not tapped out just yet. We've survived five U.S. presidents, two of them Bushes. We've endured the passing of two beloved cast members (Marcia Wallace and Phil Hartman) and four terrific writers (Sam Simon, Kevin Curran, Don Payne, and Sandy Frank). *Simpsons* writer Brian Kelley remarked, "These things are bound to happen when a show's been on infinite years."

Even if the day comes that Fox cancels us, there's the inevitable pickup by Netflix, followed by cancellation on Netflix, then brief runs on Hulu, Crackle, Seeso, Bumbum, Tooter . . . now I'm just making words up. And then there will be the *Simpsons* reboots and spin-offs . . . and some awful Broadway musical. As we stated in a catchy, stupid spoof of Billy Joel's catchy, stupid song "We Didn't Start the Fire":

> *They'll Never Stop* The Simpsons!
> *Have no fears, we've got stories for years, like*
> *Marge becomes a robot,*
> *Maybe Moe gets a cell phone, has Bart ever owned a bear?*

Why does the show endure? Because it's based on two fundamental principles: family and folly. Family is eternal. Even if Billy has two daddies, or three mommies, family never changes: it's a bunch of people stuck in one house who love each other while driving each other crazy.

As for folly, it's forever changing. Human beings are always coming up with new ways to be idiots. The newspapers are full of fresh ideas for our show: bad parenting trends for Marge, useless curriculum changes for Principal Skinner, new weapons for Chief Wiggum (oh dear), bogus but expensive medical breakthroughs for Dr. Hibbert, and innovative ways for Mayor Quimby to be corrupt and Mr. Burns to be greedy. And there will always be fresh reasons for the good people of Springfield to form an ugly mob.

When will *The Simpsons* end? The day people all over the world start treating each other with love, respect, and intelligence.

I hope that day never comes.

JUDD APATOW ON *THE SIMPSONS'* LONGEVITY

"*Simpsons* viewership may be down from what it once was, but viewership for *everything* is down. Viewership for the NFL is down! I think *The Simpsons* is still so strong. You can debate seasons and episodes, but it's as funny as anything being made right now . . . I remember six or seven years ago, people were saying, 'This might be the last year.' And then suddenly there was a moment when the world decided, 'No. We're *never* getting rid of this.'"

The Simpsons Ride at Universal Studios Florida hosted one million riders within two months of its opening in May 2008; *Theme Park Insider* named it Best New Attraction that year.

THE FINAL

BURNING QUESTION

Why are the Simpsons yellow?

I love doing *Simpsons* Q&As, because, unlike in any class I've ever taken, I've done the work and I know the answers. But at a lecture in 2009, a six-year-old boy asked me, "Why are the Simpsons yellow?"

Not only didn't I have the answer, I'd never even thought to ask the question. I went back to work and asked the other writers. They had no idea.

I finally found the answer in a candle shop in Burbank. It was hosting an art opening for a Hungarian woman who used to work for our animation house, Klasky Csupo. She was the one who received Matt Groening's original line drawings and was told to give them color. She made Marge's dress green, her hair blue, and her pearls red. (Red pearls? Where do those come from?)

There were some missteps. In early seasons, Asians were depicted with pale white skin and pink hair. But why are the Simpsons yellow? Because Bart, Lisa, and Maggie have no hairlines—there's no line that separates their skin from their hair points. So the animators chose yellow—it's kinda skin, it's kinda hair.

This doesn't explain why the Minions, SpongeBob, and Tweety Pie are all yellow. But let them write their own goddamn book.

CLOSING CREDITS

Sam Simon was asked to leave *The Simpsons* in 1993. He went on to one of the most remarkable third acts in show business history: he directed sixty TV episodes; he made money as a tournament poker player; he managed boxer Lamon Brewster, taking him from an unknown to world heavyweight champion; he spent his *Simpsons* millions feeding L.A.'s homeless, rescuing dogs, and fighting whaling. Once perceived as a prickly enfant terrible, he died as one of Hollywood's most beloved philanthropists. Sam is buried in Westwood Village Memorial Park, a compact cemetery stuffed with comedy legends: Billy Wilder, Fanny Brice, Jack Lemmon, Walter Matthau, Carroll O'Connor, Don Knotts . . .

SAM SIMON

June 6, 1955 – March 8, 2015

IT'S NOT HOW MANY TIMES YOU GET KNOCKED DOWN:
IT'S HOW MANY TIMES YOU GET BACK UP

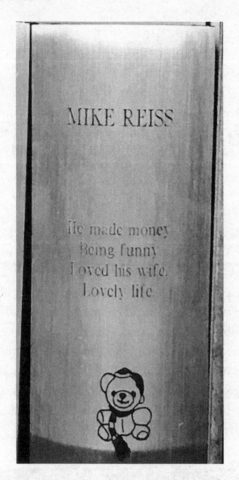

. . . and me! I'll be interred about fifty feet from Sam. My epitaph reads:

> He made money
> Being funny
> Loved his wife
> Lovely life

The teddy bear below it was my Christmas gift to Denise; the cremation urn was her gift to me.

GLOSSARY

What follows is a list of actual terms used by comedy writers. Just as language manuals use the simplest sentences ("The pen is on the table"—really?), I've chosen to illustrate them with the simplest, most obvious gags that exist: Kim Kardashian jokes.

K-words: Neil Simon's *The Sunshine Boys* exposed audiences to one of the great secrets of comedy: words with *K* sounds are funny. Cucumbers are funnier than celery. Cucamonga is funnier than Philadelphia. Kim Kardashian is funnier than anything. A warning to novices—K-words alone don't make a sentence funny. For example:

My cousin Kenny was killed by the Ku Klux Klan.

Rule of three: This is one of the few solid rules of comedy, one vouched for by scientist/*Futurama* cocreator David Cohen. The rule of three is a list joke, where the first two elements are normal, and the third element is a surprise. Example:

HE: I picked up three things at the Kim Kardashian Museum: a brochure, a T-shirt, and chlamydia.

Button: The last joke in a scene, "buttoning" it with a laugh before you move on to the next scene. Example:

> **SHE:** It's agreed, we're going out to a museum today. Which one would you like?
> **HE:** The Kim Kardashian Museum. It's always open and anyone can get in.

Act break: The moment on a TV show right before the commercial break that is so intriguing you have to stay tuned. Commercial-free sitcoms, like those on HBO, don't need act breaks, but on a network show, they are the most important part of a story pitch. Example:

> **HE:** Two tickets for the Kim Kardashian Museum.
> **GUARD:** I'm sorry, we're closed . . . There's been a murder!

Act Break

Callback: A joke repeated later in a show because it got a laugh earlier. This is a cheap, lazy trick that always seems to work. We try to avoid these on *The Simpsons*. Example:

> **SHE:** I really enjoyed the Kim Kardashian Museum.
> **HE:** We can go back tomorrow. Like I said, it's always open!

Laying pipe: Providing exposition and character detail, preferably in a subtle way. Example:

> **HE:** Let's go to that Kim Kardashian Museum. It's always open, even in this small New England town where I've come to get over my wife's unsolved disappearance that happened twenty years ago today.

Joke on a joke: When you have a perfectly decent punchline, but add another joke to it. Some writers believe this ruins the original joke; others believe it doubles the comedy. Example:

> **GRAMPA:** Let's go to that Kim Kockamamie Museum: it's always open and anyone can get in.

Wacky stack (also known as "stacking the wack"): Basically, a joke on a joke . . . on a joke on a joke. It's the hope that by stringing funny words together you will eventually strike comedy gold. You won't. Example:

> **GRAMPA:** Let's go to the Kim Kockamamie Museum. It's run by a stuttering Albanian on Dingle Street in Sheboygan.

M.O.S: Dialogue near the end of an episode where it suddenly switches from cheap jokes to unearned sentimentality. (M.O.S. stands for "Moment of Shit.") Example:

> **HE:** You know the sexiest thing in the Kim Kardashian Museum? You.
> **SHE:** Oh, honey . . .
>
> *They hug.*

Treacle cutter: After the Moment of Shit, a joke is tacked on to cut through the sweetness. Example:

> **HE:** You know the sexiest thing in the Kim Kardashian Museum? You.
> **SHE:** Oh, honey . . .
>
> *They hug. Then:*

SHE: Your keys are poking me.

HE: Those aren't keys.

Comedy killer: A word or phrase so depressing—such as bone cancer or Armenian genocide—that it kills any joke it touches. Example:

HE: Let's go to the Kim Kardashian Museum. It's always open and anyone can get in unless they have full-blown AIDS.

Nakamura: When a joke in a script bombs with an audience, and the writer knows there are four more callbacks to that same joke. Coined by Garry Marshall, after a running joke about a Mr. Nakamura went 0-for-6 with a studio audience. Example:

Ending a book with a dozen Kim Kardashian jokes.

It's 1990 and *The Simpsons* wins its first Emmy. *(Left to right, back row:)* Richard Sakai, Sam Simon, James L. Brooks, Matt Groening, Larina Adamson, David Silverman, Margot Pipkin. *(Front row:)* the rarely photographed John Swartzwelder, me, Gábor Csupó, Al Jean.

ANSWERS TO NPR PUZZLES

1. virgin wool, Virginia Woolf
2. Eva Gabor, rob a grave
3. Emma/Oliver Stone, *Mame, Oliver!*
4. Kirstie Alley; strike, alley (bowling)
5. JULianne Moore, MARianne Moore
6. Euclid, il Duce
7. Cate Blanchett, carte blanche
8. arts and crafts, carts and rafts
9. *American Idol,* Eric Idle
10. waste not, want not
11. daredevil; live, dead
12. astronomer; star, moon
13. sesame, the same

HOW DID YOU DO?

12–13 correct: Professor Frink
10–11 correct: Lisa Simpson
8–9 correct: Comic Book Guy
6–7 correct: Bart
4–5 correct: Homer
2–3 correct: Chief Wiggum
1 correct: Springfield Tire Fire
Zero correct: Ralph

ACKNOWLEDGMENTS

Mike thanks all his friends who consented to be interviewed for this thing: Judd Apatow, Nancy Cartwright, Dan Castellaneta, David Copperfield, Al Jean, Jon Lovitz, and Conan O'Brien. Thanks to Matt Klickstein for doing the interviewing—I'd never have the guts to do it. And thanks, Matt K., for conceiving this project—there wouldn't be a book without you.

Thanks to my wife, Denise, who takes more photos than most security cameras. You are the reason this book has pictures. Oh, yeah, and thanks for marrying me.

And thanks to everyone—and I mean everyone—at *The Simpsons* for letting me tell a story that really belongs to all of us. Nobody was ever resentful about it. Like I said over and over: it's a shockingly nice place to work.

Special thanks to Antonia Coffman for helping me get a pair of great *Simpsons* pics.

To anyone at *The Simpsons* I neglected to mention . . . this counts as a mention. I'm talking to you, Rob LaZebnik.

Finally, let me acknowledge that this book may contain errors, omissions, paraphrases, and exaggerations. Every story I tell is true . . . to the best of my recollection. However, I'm pushing sixty and can't even remember what I had for breakfast. (Oh, right, beer!) Plus, I do have a tendency to punch up everything, including reality.

Despite the subtitle, there is only one "Outright Lie" in the book. In chapter two, I tell a long story about my third-grade teacher, and then say it never happened. That's not true! It did happen, pretty much the way I tell it. My only lie was to lie when I said I lied. If that doesn't make sense, forgive me. I had a big breakfast.

Mathew thanks his terrific agent, Anthony Mattero at Foundry, for encouragement, counsel, friendship, and rock-hard honesty. Thanks also to Janet Rosen for her initial lessons in how to devise a winning book proposal/concept back in the "early days."

Because his last book was gratuitously crammed with an exorbitant amount of "special thanks" at the end, he'll only say here that he once again appreciates the support of his parents, friends, and family, along with all the new friends and colleagues he's come across over the past few years who have so enriched his life and made sure he'd be up to the challenge of working on yet another project with such cultural relevance . . . and all that jazz.

Brothers-in-authorship Caseen Gaines, Allen Salkin, Jon Niccum, Jai Nitz, and Adam Bradley deserve special singling-out here for hours of listening to a lot of whining and complaining, while being some of the select few on the planet who truly understand why that has to be done.

Gratitude is also due to the deliciously boho staff at Baltimore's own Baby's On Fire, at which many of the elements Mathew contributed to this project were fashioned.

Of course, he thanks Mike and Denise Reiss for their sometimes mind-boggling hospitality and generosity in opening up their lives (and in a few cases, their own home) to someone they barely knew at first.

And to all of those who contributed to this book—including interviewees (Nancy, you were my favorite)—as well as the tireless staff at Dey Street, particularly editor Matt Daddona.

Finally, Mathew has the privilege of actually doing one traditional thing in his kinetic, contrarian life and using an acknowledgment in a book to thank his wife, Becky, for being the Yoko to his Ono (bow down to the Queen of Noise), always reminding him tomorrow is another day, and at least *pretending* to laugh at all his inane jokes. *BEST. EYE ROLLING. EVER.*

IMAGE CREDITS

Photograph of the author in front of caricatures by Nevin Shalit. The Harvard Lampoon, Inc. © 1982. Used by permission.

Still of Bart in his clown bed from *The Simpsons* courtesy of Matt Groening.

Illustration of the author's brother's clown bed by John Reiss.

Image of alien lineup from *The Simpsons* courtesy of Matt Groening.

Cel of Jay Sherman from *The Critic* courtesy of Sony Pictures Television.

Still of Sid from "ICE AGE: DAWN OF THE DINOSAURS" © 2009 Twentieth Century Fox. All rights reserved.

Illustration of baby Dick by David Catrow, © 2003 by David Catrow from *The Boy Who Looked Like Lincoln* by Mike Reiss. Used by permission of Price Stern Sloan, an imprint of Penguin Publishing Group, a division of Penguin Random House LLC. All rights reserved.

Images of *Hard Drinkin' Lincoln* and Queer Duck *Time Out New York* cover courtesy of Xeth Feinberg.

Photograph of Queer Duck in Los Angeles Pride Parade courtesy of Icebox.com.

Photographs of the author with his wife, Denise Reiss, and Jennifer Tilly; the *Harvard Lampoon* building; the author in front of Johnny Carson mural; the author with Conan O'Brien; the author with Peter Jacobson; the author with Dan Castellaneta; William Friedkin and Nancy Cartwright; the author with Joel Cohen at the 2017 Emmys; *Simpsons* writers with Tom Jones; the author with "Weird Al" Yankovic; the author with Tom Arnold; the author with David Copperfield; Homer's induction into the Baseball Hall of Fame; the author on vacation; the Simpsons Ride; Sam Simon's tombstone; and the author's cremation urn by Denise Reiss.

All other photographs courtesy of the author.

ABOUT THE AUTHORS

MIKE REISS has won four Emmys and a Peabody Award during his twenty-eight years writing for *The Simpsons*. With Al Jean, he ran the show in season 4, which *Entertainment Weekly* called "the greatest season of the greatest show in history." In 2006, Reiss received a Lifetime Achievement Award from the Animation Writers Caucus.

He has written jokes for such comedy legends as Johnny Carson, Joan Rivers, Garry Shandling . . . and Pope Francis! For his comedic contributions to the charitable group Joke with the Pope, in 2015 Pope Francis declared Reiss "a Missionary of Joy."

Reiss cocreated the animated series *The Critic* and created Showtime's hit cartoon *Queer Duck* (about a gay duck), which was named one of "The 100 Greatest Cartoons of All Time" by Britain's Channel 4 viewers. *Queer Duck: The Movie* was released to rave reviews in July 2006, winning awards in New York, Chicago, San Diego, Sweden, Germany, and Wales.

He has been a contributing writer to two dozen animated films, including *Ice Age* and its four sequels, *Despicable Me* and *Despicable Me 2*, *The Lorax*, *Rio*, *Kung Fu Panda 3*, and *The Simpsons Movie*—with a worldwide gross of $11 billion.

Reiss's first full-length play, *I'm Connecticut*, set box-office records for Connecticut Repertory Theatre. The *Hartford Courant* called it "sweet" and "hysterically funny" and named it one of the year's ten best plays. BroadwayWorld Connecticut voted it Best Play of 2012. He's had five plays produced in the United States and Britain, most recently *I Hate Musicals: The Musical.*

His caveman detective story, "Cro-Magnon P.I.," won an Edgar Award from the Mystery Writers of America.

He has published eighteen children's books, including the best-seller *How Murray Saved Christmas* and the award-winning *Late for School.* Reiss also composes puzzles for NPR and *Games World of Puzzles.*

He has been happily married for thirty years. Like most children's book authors, he has no children.

MATHEW KLICKSTEIN is a writer/filmmaker whose eclectic oeuvre includes penning Sony Pictures' *Against the Dark* (Steven Seagal's only horror film to date, for good or ill), cocreating a comedic travelogue series for *National Lampoon's* short-lived television network called *CollegeTown, USA,* and cowriting/producing a gender-bending reimagining of *Lord of the Flies* as an immersive theatrical experience called *Ladies of the Fly.*

His 2013 book, *Slimed! An Oral History of Nickelodeon's Golden Age,* was included in such "Best Of" lists as those by *Entertainment Weekly, Parade,* and *Publishers Weekly.* An updated version of *Slimed!* commemorating the 40th anniversary of Nickelodeon will be released by Penguin Random House this summer. His most recent film, *On Your Marc,* chronicles the "life and slimes" of TV icon Marc Summers.

Mathew's comedic novel that lifts the veil on the modern niche of soi-disant "geek culture/media," *Selling Nostalgia,* will be published by Post Hill Press this summer as well.

As a longtime journalist, he's contributed to numerous regional, national, and online news outlets, including *Wired, New*

York Daily News, and Splitsider (now *New York Magazine's* Vulture). And he coproduces/hosts a podcast about aforementioned "nerd/geek culture" called *NERTZ* (based on his book *Nerding Out,* recently released in China) with such varied guests as Academy Award–winning screenwriter Diablo Cody, SuicideGirls founder Missy Suicide, and John Park, cocreator of the "Flo" Progressive Insurance spokeswoman.

Mathew's nationwide travels over the years have also allowed him to pursue his passion of arts therapy, working closely with persons with disabilities on filmmaking, poetry, journalism, and creative writing. These unique projects have led to partnerships with such groups as "disabled rock band" the Kids of Widney High and Denver's Phamaly, the only theater company in the country that works exclusively with actors with disabilities.

As with the vast majority of people on the planet, he's rarely if ever fiddled around much within the social media community. But if you'd like to keep up to date on his past, current, and future cartoonishly crackpot shenanigans, he does begrudgingly maintain a website at www.MathewKlickstein.com.

A few of his favorite things are *The Larry Sanders Show; Calvin and Hobbes;* the Velvet Underground; combination fried rice; his puckish wife, Becky; and highfalutin words such as "oeuvre." In fifth grade, he once got in trouble for wearing an *I'm Bart Simpson, Who the Hell Are You?* shirt to class.